# Anchoring Cultural Change and Organizational Change

A volume in
*Research on Religion and Education*
Larry Burton and Anthony J. Dosen, *Series Editors*

# Anchoring Cultural Change and Organizational Change

*Case Study Research Evaluation Project
All Hallows College Dublin 1995–2015*

## Patrick McDevitt
*DePaul Centre*

## Marjorie Fitzpatrick
*All Hallows*

INFORMATION AGE PUBLISHING, INC.
Charlotte, NC • www.infoagepub.com

**Library of Congress Cataloging-in-Publication Data**

A CIP record for this book is available from the Library of Congress
http://www.loc.gov

ISBN: 978-1-64802-154-1 (Paperback)
      978-1-64802-155-8 (Hardcover)
      978-1-64802-156-5 (E-Book)

Copyright © 2020 Information Age Publishing Inc.

All rights reserved. No part of this publication may be reproduced, stored in a retrieval system, or transmitted, in any form or by any means, electronic, mechanical, photocopying, microfilming, recording or otherwise, without written permission from the publisher.

Printed in the United States of America

# Contents

Abstract ................................................................. vii
Introduction: Research ........................................... ix
Acknowledgments ................................................... xi

**1  Historical Context** ............................................ 1
    1995–2008 ........................................................ 3
    2008–2011 ........................................................ 4
    2011–2015 ........................................................ 6

**2  Review of Literature** ........................................ 7
    Cultural Change and Organizational Change ........... 7
    The Kotter Perspective ....................................... 8
    Corporate Culture and Performance ................... 10
    Organizational Identity ..................................... 16
    Conclusion ...................................................... 20

**3  Theoretical Focus: John P. Kotter's Eight Steps** ...... 21
    Kotter's (2012) Eight Step Process "Leading Change" ...... 22
    Step 1: Establishing a Sense of Urgency ............. 23
    Step 2: Creating the Guiding Coalition .............. 24
    Step 3: Developing a Change Vision ................. 25
    Step 4: Communicating the Vision for Buy-In ..... 27
    Step 5: Empowering Broad-Based Action .......... 28

    Step 6: Generating Short-Term Wins ............................................. 29
    Step 7: Never Letting Up ................................................................. 31
    Step 8: Incorporating Changes Into the Culture ........................ 32
    Conclusion............................................................................................ 34

**4 Identity, Mission, and Organizational and Cultural Change ....... 35**
    Identity, Mission, Organization, and Cultural Change .............. 37
    Conclusion............................................................................................ 45

**5 Ethical Leadership and Organizational and Cultural Change ...... 47**
    Leadership Style and Organizational Change ............................. 50
    Conclusion............................................................................................ 56

**6 Social Justice and Organizational and Cultural Change ............... 59**
    Social Justice, Organizational and Cultural Change .................. 62
    Conclusion............................................................................................ 67

**7 Internal and External Challenges and Organizational and Cultural Change ................................................................................ 69**
    Internal and External Challenges, Organizational Change, and Cultural Change............................................................................ 71
    Conclusion............................................................................................ 77

**8 Conclusions and Recommendations................................................. 79**

**A Narrative Research: Sampling, Guideline for Questions, and Analysis Among 20 Participants ..................................................... 85**

**B Quantitative Survey (Questionnaire/Survey Monkey): Sampling, Questionnaire, and Analysis of Survey of 63 Alumni Respondents. ....................................................................... 89**

**C Quantitative Survey (Questionnaire/Survey Monkey): Sampling, Questionnaire, and Analysis of Survey of 37 Staff/Stakeholders.......................................................................... 95**

**D Documentary Research: Sampling, Documents Researched, and Analysis of 23 Documents......................................................... 103**

**E Case Study Research Evaluation................................................... 107**

**F John Kotter's Eight Step Process "Leading Change!"............................................................................... 109**

    **References ......................................................................................... 111**

# *Abstract*

In May 2014, the staff of All Hallows College (Drumcondra, Dublin, Ireland) was informed by the trustees that, due to serious financial difficulties, the college had no other option than to "wind down" the college by 2017 at the latest.

This book describes the organizational processes and changes coupled with leadership changes over three distinct eras from 1995–2015. It illustrates the challenges the college faced, and the actions taken to resolve issues and make changes. The successes and the barriers encountered as the organization worked toward solutions to the many interrelated and confounding social and financial issues with which the college was facing, are also described.

In the study, John Kotter's (2012) Steps of Organizational Change and Culture is the theoretical context in the analysis of data. Kotter (2012) stresses the point that in organizational change the "culture" must be anchored in order for change to take place successfully. Kotter understands culture as the organization's identity and the organization's attitude for change. The concept of culture also includes how identity and change interrelate to one another. Unfortunately, this anchoring of culture does not often happen in many organizations, leading to failure and the death of organizations. In general, Kotter's theory is typically used in for-profit organizations, whereas the All Hallows College (AHC) study applies Kotter's theory to a faith-based and nonprofit organization.

The study shows through narrative, documentary, quantitative, and qualitative research data that there was knowledge of the issues and challenges facing the college for decades. However, this awareness among the administration, staff, governors, and trustees of the college did not translate into the needed urgency for organizational change. Although AHC enjoyed 172 years of educational contributions to the Church and society, the study will illustrate how legacy challenges, sense of complacency, and lack of identity at *critical* times of change failed to inculcate and anchor an organizational culture and identity for change.

# Introduction: Research

*There is nothing more difficult to take in hand, more perilous to conduct,
or more uncertain in its success than to take the lead in the introduction
of a new order of things.*
—Nichollo Machiavelli (1531)

In May of 2014, it was publicly announced that All Hallows College, Dublin Ireland would begin a formal wind down of its operations due to severe financial difficulties. The college would be closed once all the enrolled students completed their programs. Following this announcement, members of the college staff were invited to carry out a case study research evaluation project. The project looked at the organizational, cultural, and leadership changes over the past 20 years in All Hallows College. The research question driving this case study was: "Why is anchoring cultural change an important component of organizational change?"

## Aim of Research

To examine the relationship between cultural change and organizational change in All Hallows College–Dublin, over 20 years (1995–2015).

## Objectives

1. To illustrate the factors (both positive and negative) influencing cultural change (e.g., identity, finance, mission, and ethos).
2. To illustrate the Vincentian social justice value influencing cultural change.
3. To evaluate the role of leadership in cultural and organizational change.
4. To determine the external and internal challenges to cultural change.

## Research Methodology

The research method was fourfold: First, there were twenty in-depth narrative interviews among staff spanning over three historical eras of All Hallows College: (a) Pre 1995–2008, (b) 2008–2011, and (c) 2011–2015. Second, a survey was conducted among a stratified sample of alumni over the last 20 years. Third, a survey of staff and other stakeholders was taken over the last 20 years. And, finally, documentary research was done using a sample of historical documents of the college over the last 20 years (see Appendices).

# Acknowledgments

The *Case Study Research Evaluation Project: All Hallows College, Dublin, 1995–2015*, would not have been made possible without the valuable professional contributions of Dr. Catherine Breathnach, Cora Lambert, Mary McPhillips, and Dr. Javan Ridge who carried out the research. A special word of gratitude is given to all the participants in the research—those who gave their time relating their narratives, those students and staff/stakeholders who took part in the two surveys, and those who wrote the documents relating to the research.

# 1

## *Historical Context*
*Pre 1995–2008*

In 1842, Father John Hand, a priest of the Meath Diocese in Ireland, purchased the lease of the All Hallows grounds and founded a missionary college for the English-speaking international missions. His idea was to provide Irish priests for many thousands of Irish emigrants going abroad during the famine years. All Hallows College (AHC) was originally and for much of its history, a seminary for the education and formation of priests (Rafferty, 2006). All Hallows College has been administered by the Vincentian Fathers and continues the Vincentian tradition. The college is a learning community committed to the mission of Jesus Christ and the education and development of people. Its core Vincentian values are ethical leadership, social justice, and service.

The years 1982–1995 were a time of transition for AHC. The college moved from being a seminary to being an institute for mission and ministry. The transition to an institute allowed lay students both men and women who were not studying for the priesthood to attend AHC. Fr. Kevin Rafferty, rector of AHC during these years, saw new possibilities opening up for the college, while at the same time the future of the college as a missionary seminary was in question. In 1982, both inside and outside Ireland, many theological and sociological changes were taking place in the Church and in society that impacted on the college's enrollment, finances, and its educational and mission relevance.

In 1983, Fr. Tom Curran, a Columban Father working in Peru, returned to Ireland on sabbatical and was asked to carry out an evaluation of the situation in AHC. We are told in *All Hallows Studies* (Rafferty, 2006) that the terms of reference were:

> Investigate and evaluate the formation for ministry in All Hallows College in relation to the needs of the Church today, the developing concept of ministry, and the traditional mission of All Hallows to go teach all nations. (pp. 144–145)

The main conclusions of Curran's (1983) research were:

1. Sources of priestly vocations were drying up in Irish society; however, AHC should continue its traditional task of preparing diocesan priests for overseas missions.
2. There was state recognition in Ireland for the AHC courses through the National Council for Educational Awards (NCEA) and Church recognition for baccalaureate degrees from the Pontifical University of St. Patrick's College Maynooth. It was Curran's recommendation that AHC explore the possibility of degree validation from other institutions of higher education such as Trinity College Dublin and Louvain College in Belgium.
3. Pastoral education was a major strength for AHC and should continue to build its programs on this strength.
4. The considerable resources of the college, such as its teaching staff, geographical location in the heart of the city of Dublin, and the easy access transportation should be continually built upon.
5. The retreat/conference center should be maximized as a resource and further its outreach to people both in Ireland and internationally.

In 1988, All Hallows Seminary became the Institute for Mission and Ministry where it continued to prepare seminarians for priestly ministry. At that time, it was also realized that the changes in the Church and society defined the need to initiate courses for laymen and laywomen. This was a catalyst in the history of AHC. For the first time in AHC's history, seminarians and lay students were studying together and pursuing the same academic degrees. The undergraduate degree course offerings at AHC had theology as the main component and the choice of three subsidiary subjects: philosophy, psychology, or spirituality. Some years later English literature was added to these options.

In the 1990s, AHC began to design alternative programs for both traditional-aged students as well as mature students. For example, undergraduate programs were offered in the evenings for many older people to follow through on adult religious education which they had no interest in as younger people or did not have the opportunity to pursue. In 1993, graduate (master's) degrees in pastoral theology and other master's degrees were introduced, followed by graduate degrees in research.

The theology of mission and ministry had gone through many developments in the post-Vatican II Church, reflected in Pope John Paul's *Christifidelis Laici* (1988), *Redemptoris Missio* (1987), and *Pastores Dabo Vobis* (1992). By the middle of the 1990s, AHC was equipped to respond to the changing times in the Church and society. The college had become more than just a seminary. The college was evolving and well on its way to become a liberal arts college and a university. It was clear that parish communities in the Western world depended on the availability of theologically and pastorally educated priests and lay ministers with a strong sense of mission.

## 1995–2008

In 1995, Fr. Mark Noonan CM took over as president of AHC from Fr. Kevin Rafferty who was named the Vincentian Provincial. In this same year, it was announced that Dublin City University (DCU) would now validate AHC degrees. In addition, there were a number of new degree programs introduced including pastoral placements for students to gain experience working in the community. In the late 1990s the name was changed from the Institute of Mission and Ministry to AHC, reflecting the changing realities that AHC was doing more than training ministers (Rafferty, 2006).

The main organizational changes from 1995–2008 were as follows:

1. The volunteer culture disappeared. For many years previously, AHC had depended on the volunteer service of Diocesan priests, men of religious congregations including the Vincentians, and sisters from different religious orders. They worked tirelessly and gave committed dedicated service for minimum salary/stipends.
2. As religious men and women began to retire they had to be replaced by lay people with reasonable salaries.
3. There was an inability to attract larger numbers of students to make the academic programs viable; hence, funding became a major issue.

4. There was no official Church recognition for the work of AHC and this hindered progress.
5. A big organizational change was the introduction of the Adult Learning Bachelor of Arts program (known as ALBA) which attracted large numbers of older students but at an unrealistically low cost to the students. The financial structure of the program depended on donations and grants from outside sources. Although the program was very effective, it failed to generate the necessary income for the program to be sustained.

## 2008–2011

This era was highly significant in the life of AHC. Because AHC was privately funded, a perilous financial situation emerged (even before 2008), that is, operating the college in a deficit with less income and greater expenses. The college was depending more and more upon donations, investments, and its endowment principle to cover necessary operational expenses. The monies raised from fundraising went into general operations instead of the endowment and other developmental investments. The remaining deficit was financed out of the principle of the college endowment. Consequently, the years of financing the deficit through developments and the endowment began to erode and have a catastrophic impact upon the financial infrastructure as well as other infrastructures, that is, facilities, programs, personnel, etc. All Hallows was going to be in financial trouble and unsustainable unless funding came from the Irish government.

In the years 2005–2006, All Hallows College had low student enrollment and a growing financial deficit. College leadership realized that as a private Catholic institution offering such courses as theology, spirituality, and Christian leadership, the college would not survive without government funding. Therefore, the college trustees made a decision to initiate talks with DCU with a view to become a "linked" college (now termed "linked provider"). In the minds of the Trustees, the link with DCU would provide the needed support and resources to sustain the college into the future.

The linkage agreement between AHC and DCU signed in 2008 offered a hopeful future for the beleaguered AHC. DCU had already validated and accredited all the degrees (many of them unique to AHC) in AHC since 1995. With this linkage agreement it was hoped there would be funding on a regular basis from the government. However, core funding from the government was not to be. Coupled with the beginning of the recession/financial crash of 2008 in Ireland and the publishing of the government's

*National Strategy for Higher Education for 2030* (Hunt, 2010), which specifically targeted the closing of small colleges, it seemed that it was the beginning of the end for AHC. At this time, there was pressure to amalgamate educational institutes and by doing so increase resources.

As a college of DCU, AHC was linked to the Faculty of Humanities and Social Sciences at the university. All Hallows College was organized into three schools: an undergraduate school, postgraduate school, and a school for adult and community education.

The major organizational changes around this time were as follows:

1. changing from a seminary/institute of mission and ministry to a college of a university;
2. the need for a formal human resource unit to be set up in AHC that had not happened before;
3. agreed procedures and practices were made more formalized between the college and the university; and
4. the research strategy of the college consisted of expertise for the doctoral programs in AHC coming from outside third-level institutions. All Hallows did not have the staff to manage the number of research students. Consequently, the costs of the doctoral programs were more expensive than if administered by the staff of AHC.

All Hallows College was Catholic in mission and values but financially independent of the Church. The college also had independence from the State. This independence was both a major strength as well as a weakness. The strength of the independence was the freedom to respond without hindrance to the critical needs of today's world in creative and imaginative ways. But, at the same time, the independence was a weakness because of the lack of resources and regular funding from Church or State. The principle source of funding for the college came in the way of student fees. As time went on, the pressure to survive brought division and questions among AHC's staff and constituencies with regard to the mission and direction of the college. A dilemma arose among the college staff about continuing as before in the tradition of seminary and ministry training. Could this model be financially sustainable? On the other hand, could the model be adapted and become part of a larger university? If so, can the college merge with an institution with different values and ethos? And, in doing so, can AHC maintain its Vincentian values of social justice, ethical leadership, and service?

## 2011–2015

In 2011, AHC saw the appointment of new president, Fr. Patrick McDevitt CM, PhD—recruited from DePaul University in Chicago. The trustees of AHC all agreed that in a new administration at AHC it was best to keep the Vincentian connection if at all possible. Fr. Eugene Curran, an Irish Vincentian became a vice president and a number of other Vincentians still taught in the college. According to Fr. Tom Dalzell (2014) in *Colloque* (2014),

> Fr. McDevitt has raised the Vincentian profile of the college. His leadership has been marked by a drive to clarify the college's identity now, to strengthen its financial viability, and to make its structured fit for purpose. All programs now focus on leadership and service and so, drawing on his experience at DePaul University in Chicago, he has introduced community-based service learning, among other things, as an essential component of the curriculum. All Hallows is more international than ever before and a new strategic plan, *Aisling 2017*, promises great things for the future.
>
> Much has changed since the idea of a missionary college of All Hallows was conceived by Fr. John Hand (1842), not least in our theological understandings of Church and mission and their relationship to society. All Hallows is faced with new challenges, particularly in terms of uncertainties in the higher education landscape in the country. But its success to date has been due to its ability to adapt to changes in the world it has sought to serve. It remains committed to the mission it had in 1842, but it continues to re-invent itself (pp. 15–17).

However, this was not to be. In 2014, the staff of AHC was told that the college was to close by 2016 and that there would be phased-out redundancies. There were many reasons for this, including the financial situation and changes in organizational leadership and culture.

In the next chapter we look at various theories of cultural change and organizational change.

# 2

## Review of Literature

### Cultural Change and Organizational Change

In our case study we used John Kotter's (1996) steps to organizational change and culture. Kotter's eighth step suggests that cultural change is the key step in looking at organizational change both in a theoretical context and in the analysis of data. Many organizational theorists including J. P. Kotter have written on and researched such topics as organizational change leadership, management, mission, and cultural change (Bolman & Deal, 2008; Bridges, 2009; Christensen, 2013; Eisenbach, Watson, & Pillai, 1999; Katzenbach, Steffen, & Kronley, 2012).

In this chapter, a review of literature will be carried out to ascertain the definition of *cultural change* and *organizational change* and how each impacts on the other. *Organizational identity* and *organizational development* will also be reviewed. In relation to cultural change, Kotter's work is reviewed and then a document containing the result of an extensive set of discussions among a group of organization development consultants and internal HR staff under the auspices of the Change Affinity Group of the New Jersey

Human Resource Planning Society is also reviewed (DiGorgio & Associates, 2008). This document was written to capture key ideas exchanged. It is described as a set of notes about cultural change, summarizing the key ideas of the authors cited. Finally, Albert and Whetton's research is reviewed (Albert & Whetton, 1985).

DiGorgio and Associates (2008) began their research discussion by asking the following questions: What is cultural change? What are the major models? What is the role of executive management in cultural change? What is the role of HR in cultural change? What works and doesn't work in cultural change?

We adapted the key questions above in our four pieces of research in the case study.

## The Kotter Perspective

In Kotter's (2012) book we read the following which is summed up by the Change Affinity Group (United States). He provides definitions of *culture*, *norms of behavior*, and *shared values*. Culture refers to norms of behavior and shared values among a group of people. Norms of behavior are ways of acting that persist because they are rewarded and the group teaches these behaviors to new people, sanctioning those who do not conform. Shared values are important concerns and goals held by most people in the group: they shape group behavior.

In Kotter's model (2012), changing the culture is the last of eight steps, not the first. He writes:

> Even when there is no personality incompatibility with a new vision, if shared values are the product of many years of experience in a firm, years of a different kind of experience are often needed to create any change. That is why cultural change comes at the end of a transformation, not the beginning. Culture is not something you can directly manipulate, as if by decree. Cultural change occurs after you have successfully altered people's actions and their new behavior has produced success, which can be traced back to the new actions and behaviors. This is not to say that culture issues don't arise in the early stages of a transformation. But to try to change the culture as a first step is a bad idea—what proof do you have to offer that it's the right way to go? (p. 164)

Kotter (2012) continues to write:

> Remember, you are always trying to engender an adaptive culture, one that benefits the four main constituents: shareholders, employees, customers,

and management. This type of culture values good leadership and management. It also encourages teamwork at the top, while minimizing layers of management and bureaucracy, as well as counterproductive interdependencies. (p. 164)

## Anchoring Change in a Culture

According to Kotter (2012), this eighth step in his theory depends on the other seven steps being incorporated into the organization. He explains that cultural change comes last, not first, and is the result of a larger process. Kotter's eight steps outline the process. Lasting change in any organization depends on results of each of the eight steps. The process introduces new approaches in the organization and how it is worthwhile to change. Such a process requires a lot of dialog among people. It can result in a turnover of key people who resist change. Promotion practices need to be changed to be compatible with the new practices. New leaders should be compatible with the new culture and be champions of the new culture.

## Shallow Roots Require Constant Watering

Kotter (2012) uses an example of a technology-oriented company to illustrate the point that organizations depending on one approach need more reinforcement regarding change. As long as the new general manager was around to focus the organization constantly on speed to market and to the customer, progress was made—substantial progress. However, when the general manager retired, the company quickly regressed because the underlying cultural belief was that technology will manage the operations. Consequently, the company quickly regressed over a 2-year period.

In an organization, the less visible shared values and group norms are, the harder it is for an organization to change. Kotter (2012) believes that culture in an organization is a very powerful factor for keeping the status quo or for promoting change. Culture is powerful for three reasons: (a) individuals are selected and indoctrinated to support a given culture; (b) culture propagation occurs through the actions of hundreds or thousands of people in and outside the organization; and (c) this reinforcement happens without much awareness or conscious intent, and therefore, it is difficult to be identified, challenged, or even discussed among the ranks of the organization.

There are different culture-change scenarios, some much harder to accomplish than others (Kotter, 2012). For example, it is difficult to bring change when the core of the old culture is not incompatible with the new vision. The challenge in such situations is to slowly graft new and more productive practices onto the old ones, while at the same time eliminating inconsistent and nonproductive practices. In every change project, Kotter stresses that any organizational change must be solidly anchored in the new culture for real transformation to successfully take place. Unfortunately, this does not happen in many organizations, leading to organizations failing to achieve their mission, priorities, and goal and possibly leading to the organization dying out.

## Corporate Culture and Performance

Kotter and Haskett (1992) researched how major cultural change took place and was successful in organizations. They studied ten organizations where major cultural change was considered successful. The companies were Bankers Trust, British Airways, ConAgra, First Chicago, General Electric, ICI, Nissan, SAS, American Express TRS, and Xerox. Kotter and Haskett found that the single most important factor distinguishing organizations where cultural change was successful from those organizations that fail was competent leaders who understood organizational culture and how to manage change (DiGorgio & Associates, 2008).

The Kotter and Haskett (1992) study showed that all 10 organizations were successful in bringing about change only after leaders were appointed with a positive record for leading. These leaders made change a top priority within their organizations. Moreover, the leaders demonstrated to their organizations the close interrelationship of competition, leadership, change, strategy, and culture. Another factor which accounted for the leaders success is the fact that they all came from the outside of the organization after an early career somewhere else. Kotter and Haskett postulate that a friendly outsider's perspective is important and critical for effecting change within an organization. They write:

> In all four very large companies in our study, the change leader had spent considerable time in the company before taking over, thereby developing a good sense of the resources in the company. Complete outsiders tended to be successful at smaller companies. (p. 94)

Finally, Kotter and Haskett (1992) suggest reasons why it is difficult to change culture from the bottom up. The sheer resistance to change in an organization requires great power to overcome, and that power resides at the top. Interdependence in organizations makes it very difficult to change anything important, without changing everything. Only people at the top can lead and move beyond the resistance (Kotter & Haskett, 1992; Nadler, 1995).

David Nadler (1995) elaborates on organizational change and focuses on *discontinuous change* and offers a definition of *organizational culture*:

> "Organizational culture" is a set of commonly shared values and beliefs. It influences the behavior of people and is reflected in work practices that is, how we do things here. "Values" are the fundamental axioms or established feelings about the desirability of some quality, like innovation or individualism. "Beliefs" are perceptions about the connections of things such as events and outcomes, for example: "Hard work will be rewarded," or "challenging the boss will get you shot." Culture is reflexive: Beliefs shape behavior, but behavior also shapes beliefs. Values affect beliefs and behavior, but beliefs and behavior also affect values. (p. 96)

Nadler (1995) concludes:

> Often espoused beliefs and values are not consistent with the beliefs and values that can be inferred from observed behavior. This lack of alignment can cause great dysfunction. Most organizations are a mixture of many cultures: one in Research & Development, another in Sales, etc. External forces, historical forces, and internal forces all shape behavior. Managers can most affect internal forces—giving them a lever to change culture. (p. 154)

Nadler (1995) considers that there needs to be three critical areas to address change within an organization:

1. The vision and content of the new culture needs to be clear and well defined. This can be done by conducting an audit of the culture and asking: "What is the culture like, what needs to be changed?" Leadership is essential for formulating and communicating the new culture. And, leaders require key champions for the vision of the new culture at all levels.
2. The leverage points for change (what and how to change) need to be identified and given strategies for achieving change.
3. It is essential to note that cultural change requires change in all the key elements of organizational context: structure, business processes, measurement, appraisal, and rewards. If, in fact, all these areas are addressed, Nadler argues that cultural change will naturally be the ultimate outcome.

The formulation of a vision that sells must include the articulation of both values and expected behaviors. It is also important that values are seen in order of priories. The Senior Executives at AT&T identified values by interviewing people lower in the organization about the new values and how they saw them being implemented. This allowed the senior executives to learn more about how to implement change and understand the issues involved in the effective transformation of a culture. Another key way to assess cultural change is to observe who is getting promoted and also the people considered to be the "good guys" or the "bad guys."

Nadler (1995) discusses a critical dilemma for leadership:

> What happens to someone delivering good results but not living the new values? This is a critical dilemma for leadership. (p. 158)

DiGorgio and Associates (2008) say the change project must include support and coaching for change. But if a person refuses to change or does not change, then they must be removed from the organization. For example, the GE Company under Jack Welch was very strongly committed to having executives both get results and live the values. If for whatever reason executives did not live up to the values and did not improve their performance, they were removed from the organization.

### Tactical Choices (When and Where to Change)

Nadler (1995) writes that the culture and values of an organization are the very foundation upon which the overall change agenda rests. Therefore, the interventions for change should be carefully sequenced separately from the hardware changes. For example, sequence change initiatives should be sometime after the announcements about hardware structural and work-process changes. The approach needs bottom-up interventions, for example, education and training, meetings, forums, and so forth. Integrate change laterally from one organization to another, that is, using beta sites and skunk works to try out changes and work out the kinks. Such learning can be transferred to other sites in the organization. It is important to consult your customers about the changes. This is a very powerful tool for change and it keeps your customers informed at every level of the change project.

Collins and Porras (2005) talk about what great companies do to maintain their cultures as cult-like. This is useful to consider when beginning the project to change the culture of an organization. According to Collins and Porras, visionary companies are not easy places to work. If the ideology is not embraced or one does not fit within the organization then one is dismissed. Visionary companies have clarity of ideology, brand, and mission. These organizations tend to be tight in their profiles of personnel, elite, and not having much room for people unwilling or unsuited to their demanding standards.

Visionary companies create these elite cultures through practical, concrete things, that is, orientation and training programs, internal universities, on-the-job socialization with peers and immediate supervisors, rigorous up-through-the-ranks policies, promoting from within, and hiring young people to shape their minds from the start. The companies expose their people to pervasive myths of heroic deeds, corporate songs, cheers, and so forth. They will have light screening practices by hiring and removing people within the first few years. The incentives for advancement in the company are closely linked to one's indoctrination to core ideology. The issuing of contests, awards, and public recognition are also closely linked to core ideology. Although such organizations hold high tolerances for honest mistakes, they enact severe penalties or termination for breaching core ideology.

Edgar Schein (2010) suggests that the success of the company creates the organizational culture. Schein writes:

> Let me begin bluntly—there is no such thing as the "right" culture and culture cannot be fostered or installed. If companies are working out of a wrong set of assumptions about how things are then they fail. The right set of assumptions is imperative in creating a successful business environment and culture. The longer companies are operational and successful, the more stable and solidified the culture becomes. Pronouncements about needing to change will either be denied or cause levels of anxiety that trigger intense resistance to change. Therefore, the project of change does not work when taking on the culture directly and head on. (p. 150)

Schein (2010) provides solutions if the present culture is dysfunctional or out of line with current environmental realities. Schein notes the following solutions:

> Start with identifying what the business problem is all about. The issue is not about culture, but about the mission of the organization and whether it is being fulfilled. Second, figure out what needs to be done strategically and tactically to solve the business problem. What does the organization need to do concretely to solve problems, survive, and grow as an organization? Third, when there is clear consensus on what needs to be done, examine the existing culture to find out how present tacit assumptions would aid or hinder. Some parts of the culture may be fine, or certain subcultures within the organization may be fine. Fourth, focus on those cultural elements that will help you get to where you need to go. It is easier to build up the strengths of a culture than to change dysfunctional elements. The diversity of a culture and its subcultures almost always has strength to leverage. Fifth, identify the culture carriers who see the new direction and feel comfortable moving in

that direction. This helps create role models, these people are often found in subcultures or in marginal roles in the organization. Sixth, build change teams around the new culture carriers. Different parts of the organization, because of environmental needs, may have to go in a different direction to produce the desired changes in thinking and acting. Seventh, the top management must adjust the reward, incentive, and control systems to be aligned with the new strategy. Eighth, the structures and routine processes of the organization must also be brought into alignment with the desired new directions. (p. 365)

Edgar Schein (2010) also believes it is important to spend the necessary time and energy across many levels of the organization with task forces and change teams. The need to change culture is powered by the need for a solution to problems. For Schein, cultural change occurs only as a by-product of addressing fundamental organizational problems. If the culture prevents organizations from making the necessary changes for success, then that culture will be a destructive force. Unfortunately, this means taking difficult and radical actions on the part of leadership to eradicate the problems. Also, according to Schein (2010), "Culture is not a suit of clothes to be changed at will. The residue of past success, it is the most stable element in an organization" (p. 365).

The American Productivity and Quality Center (1997) study showed that successful organizations have cultural change. To conduct organization change requires vision, tenacity, and a long-term horizon and commitment from top management. Such change requires extensive communication with all stakeholders. Employees must be empowered and educated so they can exploit their new power. It is necessary to systematically measure progress and results. The key elements of success include leadership, cultural change, workforce involvement, education, communication, and supportive human resource systems.

The triggers for change, according to the American Productivity and Quality Center (1997), are when organizations are on the brink of disaster and engaged in change efforts and consistently rate certain triggers higher than organizations that are not in dire circumstances. The highest-ranking triggers are changing regulatory or legal environment, competition and customer dissatisfaction, and declining or increasing profit. The second-ranked triggers are declining or increasing market share, declining or increasing revenue, and technology changes. Finally, the third-ranked triggers include employee morale, merger or acquisition, and public image of quality.

Cummings and Worley (2015) propose that there is more than one definition of organizational culture to consider. The culture of an organization is found in the shared understanding of its basic assumptions, values, norms, and artifacts. These shared understandings help members make sense of the organization—how work is done and evaluated and how employees relate to each other as well as to customers and other constituencies.

Cummings and Worley submit that corporate culture is the product of long-term social learning and reflects what has worked in the past. The organizational culture can be assessed and diagnosed and change begins with the diagnosis. In addition, they provide concrete approaches to these different definitions. The *behavioral approach* is where one assesses work behaviors and describes how relationships are managed and tasks are performed. The *competing values approach* is how organizations deal with four competing values: (a) participation versus goal achievement, (b) internal focus versus external focus, (c) stability versus creativity and innovation, and (d) organic processes versus mechanistic processes. The deep assumptions approach is very difficult and time consuming to do. There is considerable debate over whether it can be done or not. Given the problems with cultural change, most practitioners in this area suggest that changes in corporate culture should be considered only after other less difficult and less costly solutions have either been applied or ruled out.

When cultural change is in its formative stages, there are some practical approaches that can be considered. First, start with a clear vision of the organization's strategy and the shared values and behaviors needed to make it work. Have the commitment of the top management because cultural change must be managed from the top. It is critical that leaders show symbolic leadership by giving examples and walking the talk. In successful cases of cultural change, leaders almost always demonstrate a missionary zeal for new values and behaviors. Manage ethical and legal issues effectively and do not promise more on the change agenda than the organization can deliver. The organizational changes must be supported within the structure through reward systems, HR systems, information systems, and leadership style. It is important to pay careful attention to the selection and socialization of newcomers, as well as the termination of those not buying into the change agenda.

Sherriton and Stern (1997) saw corporate cultural change needing formal implementation teams to successfully bring the needed change. They conclude that some of the hidden barriers to team development are managers operating as individuals when forming teams. Many times this is due to managers concerned about control and viewing consensus building as too time consuming. Members are typically not accustomed in working together as teams. They oftentimes are not comfortable and lack the necessary communication skills to make the teams work effectively. The introduction of teams while an organization is downsizing or facing threats creates forces that are antithetical to teams.

DiGorgio and Associates (2008) defined corporate culture by ritualized patterns of beliefs, values, and behaviors. They believe one can make direct assaults on cultural change. It is the environment created by management styles; philosophies; and what is said, done, and rewarded; that creates the necessary changes in corporate culture. Furthermore, the written and unwritten norms, policies, and procedures impact on the culture.

Sherriton and Stern (1997) provide a very different perspective on cultural change. They describe successful change happening in the subcultures of the organization when top-level support was either absent or sporadic. They feel that each major functional organization such as marketing or research and development has its own subculture, as do divisions and other large units of the organization. Subcultures are influenced by the overall corporate culture, but subcultures are never the same as the overall culture. There is much more freedom to change a subculture than is commonly realized or acted upon.

The research of Sherriton and Stern (1997) considered how pervasive culture was on change. They did a survey of 100 companies regarding change in the culture of their organizations. Among the companies, 15% merged, 22% were acquired, and 41% formed alliances. There were 78% of the participants reporting working in teams, 95% were involved in at least one initiative that impacted the culture significantly, and only 51% of respondents felt their organization understood the needs and issues of the culture in making changes. The survey reported only 31% of respondents felt their organization had the skills and knowledge to address organizational culture issues. Finally, there were only 36% respondents who reported that the assessing of the culture and identifying needed changes was important. But 56% of those surveyed plan to conduct training sessions for their organizations to address cultural change.

## Organizational Identity

Organizational identity is a field of study in organizational theory that seeks the answer to the question: "Who are we as an organization?" The concept was first defined by Albert and Whetton (1985) and later updated and clarified by Whetton (2006). According to Whetton, the attributes of an organizational identity are central, enduring, and distinctive/distinguishing. A central attribute is one that writes the history of the company. If this attribute were missing, the history would be different. Enduring attributes are deeply engrained in the organization, often explicitly considered sacrosanct or embedded in the organizational history. Distinguishing attributes are used by the organization to separate itself from other similar organizations, but can also set minimum standards and norms for that type of organization. In their article, "The Dynamics of Organization Status," Podolny and Phillips (1996) write about the importance of the status of an organization. They examine the growth (and decline) of organizational status which they argue is determined by two factors: past performance outcomes and the status of the organization's affiliates. The better the past performance outcomes and the higher the status of the affiliates, the greater the organization's growth in status.

Hatch and Schultz (2002) write that organizational identity is related to, but clearly separate from, organizational culture and organizational image. It assumes a larger perspective than work identity (the identity individuals assume when in a work-related context) and organizational behavior (the study of human behavior in organizational settings). Their model consists of four dynamic processes that link identity, culture, and image. They explain the four identity processes as mirroring, reflecting, expressing, and impressing. The four processes all interplay with one another and together construct the organizational identity as an ongoing conversation or dance between organizational culture and organizational images. Figure 2.1 illustrates the dynamic of these four processes working together to form the organizational identity.

From their model, Hatch and Schultz propose that members of an organization express their understandings of the culture of the organization through organizational identity that in turn affects the perceptions of

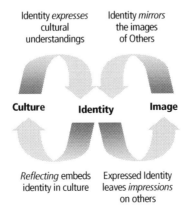

**Figure 2.1** Hatch and Schultz (2002) Organizational Identity Dynamics model.

outsiders about the organization. This outsiders' organizational "image" in turn, affects the organization's identity that again is reflected in the organization's "culture." Organizational identity can have two major influences on members: (a) It can provide an important psychological support, that is, an "anchor" as Kotter suggests, in time of change, and (b) it can also provide a possible resistance to change. Yueh-Ysen Lin (1995) suggests, in times of change, organizational identity influences management and members actions and decision-making regarding change initiatives and the interpretation of organizational events and actions. Moreover, organizational identity affects members' comparison processes and evaluation of strategies and actions as well.

Albert and Whetton (1985) define organizational identity as a set of statements that outline what is central and important to organizations, what is distinctive and unique in organizations, and what is enduring for the organization. These statements both define organizations' identity and imply that organizational change is difficult because the loss of identity will have a strong impact on the organization.

The research of Albert and Whetton (1985) suggest that an identity statement is collectively and cognitively held by organization members to answer questions such as "Who are we?"; "What business are we in?"; and "What do we want to be?" Organizational identity influences both leaders and members within an organization. For organizational leaders, organizational identity is influential on their decision-making activities within an organization. Typically, identity questions surface and attract the management's attention when they cannot find easier, more specific, and more quantifiable solutions regarding specific organizational issues. By defining the organization's identity, organizational leaders establish a fundamental base that serves as the guide for them to engage in decision-making activities.

Whetton (2006) clarified and reinforced the need to develop an organizational identity especially during times of change. The concept of identity should be formulated in such a way to be distinguished from the organization's culture and image and to be a concept that is operational. The organization's identity needs to be reflective of individual identities and structures as well as parallel distinguishing features of individual and organization identities. In the *Journal of Management Inquiry*, Whetton (2006) recommends listening to the answers to the question, "Who are we as an organization?" within the framework of a defined identity concept (what) and the associated identity-referencing discourse (how, when, why). Feldman (2002) observed that people commit to their deepest memory and dare not forget.

Whetton (2006) writes that organization identity contains three principle components ideational, definitional, and phenomenological. The *ideational* component refers to people's shared beliefs regarding who we are as an organization. The *definitional* component proposes a specific conceptual domain for the organization's identity. Finally, the *phenomenological* component theorizes identity discourse occurs in conjunction with significant and meaningful experiences within the organization. The reasons there are many different and conflicting organization identities is due to the lack of conceptual clarity. There is a common practice of treating the ideational part of our tripartite formulation as if it were the whole, and thus treating the whole as if it were its least discriminating part. The identity of an organization is specified as the central and enduring attributes that distinguish it from other organizations.

Whetton and Mackey (2002) refer to *organizational identity claims* as signifying an organization's self-determined and unique social space reflected in its unique pattern of binding commitments.

This conception of organizational identity rests on two core assumptions, extracted from organizational theory and identity theory. First, organizations are more than social collectives, in that modern society treats organizations in many respects as if they were individuals—granting them analogous powers to act and assigning them analogous responsibilities as collective social actors (Bauman, 1990; Coleman, 1974; Scott, 2003; Zuckerman, 1999). Whetton (2006) writes that this view of organizations suggests a distinction between organizational identity (the identity of a collective actor) and collective identity (the identity of a collection of actors). It also highlights important functional and structural parallels between the identity of organizational actors and individual actors (Czarniawska, 1997). Second, Whetton equates identity with an actor's subjective sense of uniqueness, referred to as the self-view or self-definition and reflected in notions such as self-governance and self-actualization. He suggests that framed in this manner, the identity of individuals and organizations is an unobservable subjective state—a causal attribution that is inferred from its posited effects or consequences, especially an actor's "identifying commitments" or "distinctive behavioral signature" (p. 219). Baumeister (1998), Baumeister and Vohs (2003), Leary and Tangney (2003), and Mischel and Morf (2003) have also written on organizational identity. In the *Administrative Scientific Quarterly*, Rao, Davis, and Ward (2000) stated, "Organizations acquire a social identity from the industry to which they belong, the organizational form they use, and through membership in accrediting bodies" (p. 270).

Finally, Whetton (2006) acknowledges that it naturally follows that widely shared negative characterizations of an organization (e.g., highly bureaucratic) may explain member turnover, they do not constitute an organizational-identity explanation of member turnover. He observes "that enduring definitional standard, legitimate identity claims are, generally speaking, those elements that have withstood the test of time" (p. 224).

## Conclusion

The concept of organizational culture is defined and used as a system of shared assumptions, values, and beliefs which govern how people behave in organizations. Organizational identity refers to a set of statements that organization members perceive to be central, distinctive, and enduring to the organization. The concept of change is about different and more effective strategies, processes, procedures, technologies, and culture, as well as the effect such changes have on the organizations. The ethos is derived from the Greek word meaning "character"; used to describe the guiding beliefs or ideals that characterize a community, nation, or ideology. The ethos of an organization is a core set of values or operating principles that are used to set the tone of the organization's overall operations. The mission of organizations brings together every element of the organization and is the energy, commitment, and passion that give the organization purpose and ultimate meaning.

It is necessary to look at both the identity of an organization as well as the identity within an organization. It cannot be that all institutionalized organizational features qualify as identity referents, but all identity referents must be institutionalized features of an organization. One of the most difficult aspects of framing organizational identity from the perspective of an organizational actor is properly accounting for the subjective ("I") frame of reference. At the core of identity theory, the persistent questions must be asked: "Who speaks for an organization?" and "Who gets to specify an organization's identity?" The responses offered direct the attention away from the "who" to the "when," "how," and "why" of identity-revealing organizational discourse. Having argued that identity referents are known by the distinctive functions they perform, the distinctive way in which they are structured, and the distinctive organizational circumstances that provoke their use, the proposed conception of organizational identity lends itself to model building, hypothesis testing, and empirical measurement.

# 3

## *Theoretical Focus*

### *John P. Kotter's Eight Steps*

In 1996, John P. Kotter wrote a book entitled *"Leading Change"* which was based on his research into mainly profit-based organizations in the United States. In 2012, he published a follow-up book by the same title. This book contained a new preface. Kotter (2012) writes in this preface:

> The material in this book is not only relevant now, sixteen years after it was published, but I believe it is *more* relevant, and for one simple reason: the speed of change continues to increase. (p. vii, emphasis in original)

He continues,

> The most fundamental mistakes smart people make when they are trying to make big changes, especially implementing high stakes strategies or initiatives, are mostly still the same today. (p. vii)

Kotter (2012) makes an important point that management is *not* leadership although the concept is better understood today, but not nearly as well as is needed. He writes,

> Management makes a system work. It helps you do what you know how to do. Leadership builds systems or transforms old ones. It takes you into a territory that is new and less well known or completely unknown to you. This point has huge implications in an ever-faster-moving world. (p. vii)

Kotter concludes this preface by advising that speed of change is the driving force. Leading change competently is the only answer. Although Kotter carried out research into profit-making organizations, our case study is about a non-profit organization involved in education and which has unfortunately had to wind down. The rationale for using Kotter's process of eight steps is that it seems to be the most appropriate context within which to place our research and in particular the analysis of our results.

## Kotter's (2012) Eight Step Process "Leading Change"

*Step 1: Establishing a Sense of Urgency.* Help others see the need for change and they will be convinced of the importance of acting immediately.

*Step 2: Creating the Guiding Coalition.* Assemble a group with enough power to lead the change effort and encourage the group to work as a team.

*Step 3: Developing a Change Vision.* Create a vision to help direct the change effort and develop strategies for achieving that vision.

*Step 4: Communicating the Vision for Buy-In.* Make sure as many as possible understand and accept the vision and the strategy.

*Step 5: Empowering Broad-Based Action.* Remove obstacles to change; change systems or structures that seriously undermine the vision; and encourage risk-taking and nontraditional ideas, activities, and actions.

*Step 6: Generating Short-Term Wins.* Plan for achievements that can easily be made visible, follow-through with those achievements and recognize and reward employees who were involved.

*Step 7: Never Letting Up.* Use increased credibility to change systems, structures, and policies that don't fit the vision; also hire, promote, and develop employees who can implement the vision; and finally, reinvigorate the process with new projects, themes, and change agents.

*Step 8: Incorporating Changes Into the Culture.* Articulate the connections between the new behaviors and organizational success and develop the means to ensure leadership development and succession (p. 23, p. 36).

The case study of All Hallows College (AHC) looks back over 20 years and focuses on organizational change over three eras of leadership/management.

The four pieces of research methodology in the case study used the abovementioned eight steps in Kotter's process, both in the questions and also in the analysis of the results.

## Step 1: Establishing a Sense of Urgency

Help others see the need for change and they will be convinced of the importance of acting immediately.

Kotter (2012) suggests that any major change in an organization can be "very, very tough." He writes:

> Whether taking it [organization] that is on its knees and restoring it to health or improving things within, the work requires great cooperation, initiative, and willingness to make sacrifices from many people often above and beyond what is seen as the normal call. Therefore, a sense of urgency is crucial to gaining needed cooperation. In other words where complacency is high, transformations go nowhere. Where there is low urgency, the momentum for change will probably die far short of the finish line. (p. 37)

Kotter (2012) writes that "people will find a thousand ingenious ways to withhold cooperation from a process that they sincerely think is unnecessary or wrongheaded" (p. 38). Sometimes people are not inclined to admit that problems exist and if they do, they cannot do anything about changing the situation or, alternatively, they do not want to do anything about the situation. The attitude can exist that it is management's problem not mine.

Sources of complacency suggested by Kotter (2012) are: (a) the absence of a major crisis; (b) too many visible resources; (c) low overall performance standards; (d) organizational structures that focus employees on narrow functional goals; (e) internal measurement systems that focus on the wrong performance indexes; (f) a lack of sufficient feedback from external sources; (g) a kill-the-messenger-of-bad-news, low candor, low confrontation culture; (h) human nature with its capacity for denial, especially if people are already busy or stressed; and (i) too much happy talk from senior management (pp. 53–54). Kotter's advice in this regard is: "Never underestimate the magnitude of the forces that reinforce complacency and that help to maintain the status quo" (p. 58).

In creating a strong sense of urgency, good leadership is demanded. If top management consists only of cautious managers unwilling to take risks, no one will push the urgency rate sufficiently high and a major transformation will never succeed. It is important in every organization that considerable change is always ongoing and absolutely essential for the ultimate success of the organization in this fast-moving world.

## Step 2: Creating the Guiding Coalition

Assemble a group with enough power to lead the change effort and encourage the group to work as a team.

Kotter (2012) writes:

> Because major change in an organization is so difficult to accomplish, a powerful force is required to sustain the process. No one individual is ever able to develop the right vision, communicate it to large numbers of people, eliminate all the key obstacles, generate short-term wins, lead and manage dozens of change projects, and anchor new approaches deep in the organization's culture. (pp. 53–54)

Kotter (2012) further suggests that in today's business environment only teams with the right composition and sufficient trust among members can be highly effective under new circumstances. He writes, "A guiding coalition that operates as an effective team can process more information, more quickly and make decisions based on the information during a major transformation" (p. 58). It can also speed the implementation of new approaches because powerful people are truly informed and committed to key decisions.

Kotter (2012, p. 58) postulates that putting together the guiding coalition involves:

1. *Position Power:* Are there enough key players on board, especially main managers, so that those left out cannot easily block progress?
2. *Expertise:* Are there various points of view—in terms of discipline, work experience, nationality, and so forth—relevant to the task at hand, adequately represented so that informed, intelligent decisions will be made?
3. *Credibility:* Does the group have enough people with good reputations in the firm so that its pronouncements will be taken seriously by other employees?
4. *Leadership:* Does the group include enough proven leadership to be able to drive the change process? You need both management

and leadership skills on the guiding coalition, and they must work in tandem, teamwork style. The former keeps the whole process under control, while the latter drives the change.

Teamwork on a guiding coalition can be created in many ways. But, regardless of the process used, one component is necessary: trust. When trust is present, people are able to create team environments. On the contrary, when trust is lacking, teams cannot be created.

Kotter (2012) advises in order to make change happen:

> The combination of trust and a common goal shared by people with the right characteristics can make for a powerful team. The resulting guiding coalition will have the capacity to make needed change happen despite all the forces of inertia. It will have the potential, at least, to do the hard work involved in creating the necessary vision, communicating the vision widely, empowering a broad base of people to take action, ensuring credibility, building short-term wins, leading and managing dozens of different change projects, and anchoring the new approaches in the organization. (p. 68)

## Step 3: Developing a Change Vision

Create a vision to help direct the change effort and develop strategies for achieving that vision.

Two major approaches in attempting to make changes in an organization should be avoided: (a) authoritarian decree, and (b) micromanagement. Kotter (2012) elaborates:

> Authoritarian decree—without the power of Kings and Queens behind it, authoritarianism is unlikely to break through all the forces of resistance. People will ignore you or pretend to cooperate while doing everything possible to undermine your efforts. Micromanagement—tries to get around this problem by specifying what employees should do in detail and then monitoring their compliance. This tactic can break through some of the barriers to change, but in an increasingly unacceptable amount of time. Because the creation and communication of detailed plans is deadly slow, the change in this way tends to be highly incremental. (p. 70)

Kotter (2012) suggests that the only approach which has the approach to break through all the forces that support the status quo and encourage the kind of dramatic shifts found in successful transformations is one which is based on vision—a central component of all great leadership. *Vision* according to Kotter refers to a picture of the future with some implicit or explicit commentary on why people should strive to create that future. In a change process, a good vision has three components:

1. Clarifying the direction of change simplifies hundreds or thousands of more detailed decisions
2. Vision serves to facilitate major changes by motivating action that is not necessarily in people's short-term self-interests. Usually, this can involve some pain. But the price of a better future is small. For example, people might be asked to work outside their comfort zone, or work with fewer resources, asked to learn new skills and behaviors and threatened with the possibility of job loss. A good vision will help to motivate people to make some sacrifices which will eventually yield particular benefits and personal satisfactions that are far superior to those available today, or tomorrow, without attempting to change.
3. Vision helps to align individuals, thus coordinating the actions of motivated people in a remarkably efficient way (pp. 71–72).

Without a shared sense of direction, interdependent people can end up in constant conflict and nonstop meetings. With a shared vision, they can work with some degree of autonomy and yet not trip over each other. Kotter (2012) suggests the following characteristics of an effective vision include:

- imaginable
- desirable
- feasible
- focused
- flexible
- communicable (p. 74).

Kotter (2012) advises:

Reengineering, restructuring, and other change programs never work well over the long run unless they are guided by visions that appeal to most of the people who have a stake in the enterprise: employees, customers, stockholders, suppliers, communities. A good vision can demand sacrifices from some or all of these groups in order to produce a better future, but it never ignores the legitimate long-term interests of anyone. (p. 75)

In order to create an effective vision Kotter (2012) writes:

*First draft:* The process often starts with an initial statement from a single individual reflecting both his or her dreams and real marketplace needs.

*Role of the guiding coalition:* The first draft is always modeled over time by the guiding coalition or an even larger group of people.

*Importance of teamwork:* The group process never works well without a minimum of effective teamwork.

*Role of the head and the heart:* Both analytical thinking and a lot of dreaming are essential throughout the activity.

*Messiness of the process:* Vision creation is usually a process of two steps forward and one back, movement to the left and then to the right.

*Time frame:* Vision is never created in a single meeting. The activity takes months, sometimes years.

*End product:* The process results in a direction for the future that is desirable, feasible, focused, and flexible and is conveyable in 5 minutes or less. (p. 84)

A final word from Kotter (2012) on *Vision*:

A vision can be mundane and simple, at least partially, because in successful transformations it is only one element in a larger system that also includes strategies, plans and budgets. (p. 73)

## Step 4: Communicating the Vision for Buy-In

Make sure as many as possible understand and accept the vision and the strategy.

Kotter (2012) writes:

The real power of a vision is unleashed only when most of those involved in an enterprise or activity have a common understanding of its goals and direction. That shared sense of a desirable future can help motivate and coordinate the kinds of actions that create transformation. (p. 87)

Gaining understanding and commitment to a new direction is never an easy task. Therefore, it is of major importance to communicate the vision to all. Not that alone, but also to ensure that as many as possible understand and accept the vision and strategy. Two ways communication is ineffective is when the vision is communicated too broadly (senior management can seem to communicate the message but there is so much information that employees are overwhelmed with the information and choose to ignore it); and communicated often, but poorly. To demonstrate this, Kotter (2012) provides us with one such communication:

> Our goal is to become the first truly transnational firm at the conjunction of the converging communication/information industries to achieve a boundary less organization and a paradigm shift strategy. (p. 88)

Kotter (2012) provides us with the key elements for effective communication of vision:

> *Simplicity:* All jargon and techno-babble must be eliminated.
> *Metaphor, analogy and example:* A verbal picture is worth a thousand words.
> *Multiple forums:* Big meetings and small memos and newspapers and formal and informal interaction—all are effective for spreading the word.
> *Repetition:* Ideas sink in deeply only after they have been heard many times.
> *Leadership by example:* Behavior from important people that is inconsistent with the vision overwhelms other forms of communication.
> *Explanation of seeming inconsistencies:* Unaddressed inconsistencies undermine the credibility of all communication.
> *Give-and-take:* Two-way communication is always more powerful than one-way communication. (p. 92)

Kotter advises that two-way communication is necessary for communicating the vision and an essential method for helping people answer all the questions that occur to them in a transformation effort.

## Step 5: Empowering Broad-Based Action

Remove obstacles to change, change systems or structures that seriously undermine the vision, and encourage risk-taking and nontraditional ideas, activities, and actions.

Environmental change demands organizational change. Major internal transformation rarely happens unless many people assist. Yet employees generally won't help, or can't help, if they feel relatively powerless. Hence, this concept determines the relevance of "empowerment" for the employees. The purpose of Step 5, according to Kotter (2012), "is to empower a broad base of people to take action by removing as many barriers to the implementation of the change vision as possible in this point in the process" (p. 106).

> **BARRIERS TO EMPOWERMENT:**
>
> Bosses discourage actions which encourage change
>
> Employers understand the vision and the needed actions aimed at the vision and want to make it a reality, but a lack of skills undermines implementing the new vision.
>
> Personnel and Information systems make it difficult to act.
>
> Formal structures make it difficult to act.

Kotter (2012) suggests the following ways to empower people to effect change:

- *Communicate a sensible vision to employees:* If employees have a shared sense of purpose, it will be easier to initiate actions to achieve that purpose.
- *Make structures compatible with the vision:* Unaligned structures block needed action.
- *Provide the training employees need:* Without the right skills and attitudes, people feel disempowered.
- *Align information and personnel systems to the vision:* Unaligned systems also block needed action.
- *Confront supervisors who undercut needed change:* Nothing disempowers people the way a bad boss can (p. 119).

Kotter (2012) advises

> that discouraged and disempowered employees never make enterprises winners in a globalizing economic environment. But with the right structure, training, systems, and supervisors to build on a well-communicated vision, increasing numbers of firms are finding that they can tap an enormous source of power to improve organizational performance. They can mobilize hundreds or thousands of people to help provide leadership to produce needed changes. (p. 119)

## Step 6: Generating Short-Term Wins

Plan for achievements that can easily be made visible, follow-through with those achievements and recognize and reward employees who were involved. Kotter (2012) writes, "that major changes take time, sometimes lots of time. Running a transformation effort without serious attention to short-term wins is extremely risky" (p. 196).

Also, according to Kotter (2012), a good short-term win has at least these three characteristics:

- It is visible—large numbers of people can see for themselves whether the result is real or just hype.
- It's unambiguous—there can be little argument over the call.
- It's clearly related to the change effort.

Kotter (2012) further writes that the role of short-term wins is to

- *Provide evidence that sacrifices are worth it:* Wins greatly help justify the short-term costs involved.
- *Reward change agents with a pat on the back:* After a lot of hard work, positive feedback builds morale and motivation.
- *Help fine-tune vision and strategies:* Short-term wins give the guiding coalition concrete data on the viability of their ideas.
- *Undermine cynics and self-serving resisters:* Clear improvements in performance make it difficult for people to block needed change.
- *Keep bosses on board:* Provides those higher in the hierarchy with evidence that the transformation is on track.
- *Build momentum:* Turns neutrals into supporters, reluctant supporters into helpers, etc. (p. 127).

Kotter (2012) provides a table which he labels as The Relationship of Leadership, Management, Short-Term Results, and Successful Transformation (see Table 3.1). Kotter advises that charismatic leaders can often be poor managers and if a poor manager doesn't value management skill in

**TABLE 3.1 The Relationship of Leadership, Management, Short-Term Results, and Successful Transformation**

| Charismatic Leaders and Good Management | Charismatic Leaders and Poor Management |
|---|---|
| L. Transformation efforts can be successful. All highly successful transformation for a while but often fail after short-term with good management efforts combine good leadership results become erratic. | L. Transformation efforts go nowhere. Short-term results are possible especially through cost-cutting or mergers and acquisitions. But real transformation programs have trouble getting started and major long-term change is rarely achieved. |

*Note:* L = Leadership
*Source:* p. 134

others, achieving short-term wins will be problematic at best. Where charismatic leaders are good managers the reverse is true.

Kotter (2012) concludes this chapter by writing:

> In a way, the primary purpose of the first six phases of the transformation process is to build up sufficient momentum to blast through the dysfunctional granite walls found in so many organizations. When we ignore any of these steps, we put all our efforts at risk. (p. 135)

## Step 7: Never Letting Up

Use increased credibility to change systems, structures, and policies that don't fit the vision; also hire, promote, and develop employees who can implement the vision; and finally, reinvigorate the process with new projects, themes, and change agents.

Kotter (2012) suggests that irrational and political resistance to change never fully dissipates. Kotter warns against possible resisters who for various reasons can be shrewd and cynical but seemingly approve of any "successes" at the time but gradually become very negative and less likely to continue to implement the vision and progress seems to disappear. Another warning from Kotter is that

> without much experience, we often don't adequately appreciate a crucial fact: that changing highly interdependent settings is extremely difficult because, ultimately, you have to change nearly everything. Because of all the interconnections, you can rarely move just one element by itself. You have to move dozens or hundreds or thousands of elements, which is difficult and time consuming and can rarely if ever be accomplished by just a few people. (p. 142)

Because change in highly interdependent systems often means changing nearly everything, it can take years rather than months. Here, leadership is invaluable. Outstanding leaders are willing to think long term. On the other hand, managers often think in terms of much shorter time frames.

Kotter (2012) suggests what Stage 7 looks like in a successful, major change effort:

- *More change, not less:* The guiding coalition uses the credibility afforded by short-term wins to tackle additional and bigger change projects.
- *More help:* Additional people are brought in, promoted, and developed to help with all the changes.

- *Leadership from senior management:* Senior people focus on maintaining clarity of shared purpose for the whole effort and keeping urgency levels up.
- *Project management and leadership from below:* Lower ranks in the hierarchy both provide leadership for specific projects and manage those projects.
- *Reduction of unnecessary interdependencies:* To make change easier in both the short and long term, managers identify unnecessary interdependencies and eliminate them.

## Step 8: Incorporating Changes Into the Culture

Articulate the connections between the new behaviors and organizational success and develop the means to ensure leadership development and succession.

Kotter (2012) writes that the culture of any organization is powerful. He defines culture as follows:

> Culture (corporate) refers to the "norms of behavior" and "shared values" among a group of people in an Organization. "Norms of behavior" are common or pervasive ways of acting that are found in a group and persist because group members tend to behave in ways that teach these practices to new members, rewarding those who fit in and sanctioning those who do not. "Shared Values" are important concerns and goals shared by most of the people in a group that tend to shape group behavior and that often persist over time when group membership changes. (p. 156)

Kotter writes (2012) that culture is powerful for three primary reasons:

1. Individuals are selected and indoctrinated so well.
2. The culture exerts itself through the actions of hundreds or thousands of people.
3. All of this happens without much conscious intent and thus is difficult to challenge or even to discuss (p. 159).

Kotter (2012) suggests that when new practices are grafted onto the old culture, in many transformation efforts, the core of the old culture is not incompatible with the new vision, although some specific norms will be. He writes that when new practices replace the old culture, anchoring a new set of practices in a culture is difficult enough when those approaches are consistent with the core of the culture. When they aren't, the challenge is much greater (p. 163).

Kotter's (2012) theory about culture is:

> Cultural Change comes last not first. Culture is not something that you manipulate easily. Culture changes only after you have successfully altered people's actions, after the new behavior produces some group benefits, and after people see the connection between the new actions and the performance improvement. Thus, most cultural change happens in Stage 8 not Stage 1. (p. 164)

He advises that a good rule of thumb is "whenever you hear of major restructuring, reengineering, or strategic redirection in which Step 1 is changing the culture' you should be concerned that it might be going down the wrong path" (p. 165).

Kotter (2012) continues:

> Both attitude and behavior change typically begin early in a transformation process. These alterations then create changes in practices that help a firm produce better products or servants at lower costs. But only at the end of the change cycle does most of this become anchored in the culture. (p. 166)

Kotter (2012) describes important considerations about anchoring change in a culture:

- *Comes last, not first:* Most alterations in norms and shared values come at the end of the transformative process.
- *Depends on results:* New approaches usually sink into a culture only after it's very clear that they work and are superior to old methods.
- *Requires a lot of talk:* Without verbal instruction and support, people are often reluctant to admit the validity of new practices.
- *May involve turnover:* Sometimes the only way to change a culture is to change key people.
- *Makes decisions on succession crucial:* If promotion processes are not changed to be compatible with the new practices, the old culture will reassert itself.

Kotter (2012) concludes:

> It is because such change is so difficult to bring about that the transformation has eight stages instead of two or three, that it often takes so much time, and that it requires so much leadership from so many people. (p. 166)

## Conclusion

In conclusion, Kotter (2012) suggests possible implications for the 21st century. He says that in any organization of the future there should be a persistent sense of urgency, teamwork at the top, people who can create and communicate vision, and broad-based empowerment. There should also be delegated management for excellent short-term performance, no unnecessary interdependence, and an adaptive corporate culture (pp. 170–179). Armed with John Kotter's eight step process in leading change, the next chapters describe and analyze the case study research evaluation project that was carried out at AHC–Dublin in 2016.

# 4

## Identity, Mission, and Organizational and Cultural Change

Vincentian identity and mission gets its example and inspiration from Vincent DePaul, a 17th century French priest who transformed attitudes and the micro and macro approaches in addressing poverty and other social issues. For Vincentians, identity and mission are intimately bound one to another—identity is mission and mission is the identity. Furthermore, the Vincentian identity and mission are fundamentally Catholic and are deeply rooted in the discipleship call of Jesus Christ. This Catholic source is understood as "universal" and for the salvation, progress, and liberation of the whole world. The Catholic and Vincentian identity and mission beckons people to look beyond the personal, local, and provincial needs of their communities.

Nelson Mandela (2013) encourages us to be the best we can be throughout all of our lives. There is no passion to be found in playing small—settling for a life that is less than the one you are capable of living. This universal call raises human consciousness to a higher level of reality of the interconnectedness and communion of the human family. As St. Paul of Tarsus says in the Christian Scriptures, "If one member suffers, all suffer together; if one member is honored, all rejoice together" (1 Corinthians 12:26, ESV). In Vincentian Family (2010), we are told that Vincentian values espouse the principle that only collectively can "we" make a significant and systemic difference for the world around us, especially the poor and discouraged. Therefore, the Vincentian identity and mission must care and be responsive to the needs of the whole world. The identity and mission of the Vincentian ethos is to "bring good news" and hope to all people, especially those who are most in need. This ethos is manifested first and foremost in the goodness and beauty of human relationships. Authentic and genuine human connection is true and can be disarming and transforming for people. As the Buddhist teacher, Daisaku Ikeda (2009) states, "True love should be transformative; a process that amplifies our capacity to cherish not just one person but all people."

Vincent DePaul would view this process of relationship, love, and transformation as "evangelization." Evangelization is a grace (free gift from the Divine) and an intimate human encounter and exchange with another person, community, and/or nature which opens the human heart and spirit to hope, to dreams, and infinite possibilities. The Vincentian ethos ultimately allows people to see the world and universe without limits, barriers, or divisions.

In Vincentian Family (2010) we read that the universal, relational, and hope-filled Vincentian identity and mission must be witnessed in actions of service to others and advocacy for social justice and progress. St. Augustine of Hippo (1961) said, "Love and say it with your life" (p. 8). These actions constantly address micro and macro human needs. The individual person needs to be cared for in a personal and loving manner. Moreover, the Vincentian call-to-action necessitates taking a "big picture" view of things and advocating and bringing change to oppressive and unjust systems which marginalize people. The Vincentian identity and mission does not take a conservative or cautious view of progress, it embraces an understanding that progress demands great risks and real change. Being willing to take risks and lead change means exposing oneself to the possibilities of failure, misunderstanding, conflict, and possibly persecution. And, without such risks and change, real transformation and progress are not possible.

The Vincentian approach fully acknowledges the "messiness" of the human condition and there is no "perfect way" to grow and develop. The Vincentian identity and mission commits itself in the messy struggle of humanity in achieving its dreams and goals. Such a commitment calls for a willingness to suffer for the sake of others. This identity and mission believes that suffering is redemptive and will be a transforming experience. The writer Kahlil Gibran (1908) stated, "Out of suffering have emerged the strongest souls; the most massive characters are seared with scars." To embrace such an identity and mission requires faith and courage.

This 17th century mission and identity continues to be more relevant today in addressing global issues of poverty, injustice, war, and violence in society. This is a unique time in history with crises of epic portions. However, these challenges open a new era of opportunities for fresh thinking, growth, and collaboration beyond the traditional paradigms.

The Vincentian identity and mission can provide a point of reference, vision, and inspiration for a dynamic future of progress, justice, and hope.

## Identity, Mission, Organization, and Cultural Change

While researching our book using narrative research, the factors of identity, finance, mission, and ethos of All Hallows College (AHC) were of great importance in influencing organizational and cultural change.

Our research delved into this statement and very interesting results emerged—particularly when analyzed under Kotter's stages. The following data collectively examines three eras of AHC: Era 1: Pre 1995–2008; Era 2: 2008–2011; and Era 3: 2011–2015. The rationale for using these eras is that there was a change in leadership during these three eras.

*Step 1: Establishing a Sense of Urgency.* Help others see the need for change and they will be convinced of the importance of acting immediately.

*Step 2: Creating the Guiding Coalition.* Assemble a group with enough power to lead the change effort and encourage the group to work as a team.

*Step 3: Developing a Change Vision.* Create a vision to help direct the change effort and develop strategies for achieving that vision.

*Step 4: Communicating the Vision for Buy-in.* Make sure as many as possible understand and accept the vision and the strategy.

*Step 5: Empowering broad-based action.* This involves getting rid of obstacles. Changing systems and structures that undermine the change vision. Encouraging risk taking and nontraditional ideas, activities and actions.

*Step 6: Generating Short-term Wins.* Plan for achievements that can easily be made visible, follow-through with those achievements and recognize and reward employees who were involved.

*Step 7: Consolidating gains and producing more change.* Using increased activity to change all systems, structures and policies that do not fit together and do not fit the transformation vision.

Hiring, promoting and developing people who can implement the change vision.

*Step 8: Incorporating Changes Into the Culture.* Articulate the connections between the new behaviors and organizational success and develop the means to ensure leadership development and succession.

The data from the case study carried out in AHC examined the factors of identity, finance, mission and ethos, and organizational and cultural change. The results from the case study were incorporated into Kotter's steps as outlined above.

## Era 1: Pre 1995–2008

The narrative data described disagreements and tensions among people not wanting to change from a seminary to an institution of mission and ministry.

The narrative data for Kotter's Step 3 demonstrated the college's move toward more community-based programs. There were attempts to make theology and spirituality broader and more relevant for both the Church and society. The people at AHC were proud of the college's ethos and good reputation and believed the college needed to continue.

Narrative data in the pre 1995–2008 era shows the past-men (alumni) of the seminary were not supportive of the emerging new operational culture of the college. The majority of the past-men lived outside Ireland and provided a small level of donations to the college. The service and attention given to the past-men was a high priority in the college.

The main positive short wins according to the narrative and documentary data during this era were changes and innovations to the curriculum (e.g., pastoral education and psycho-synthesis) to directly benefit students, the inclusion of the Central Applications Offers (CAO) to students who were not seminarians. The involvement of lay people and the development of lay leadership in the Church were seen as "ahead of its time." During this era the main organizational change was from seminary to an Institute of Mission and Ministry—open to the laity as well as to priests. This change was generally seen as positive. There were sufficient financial resources to support operations.

The documentary data for the pre 1995–2008 era report a significant change in direction from when AHC was a seminary. They introduced groundbreaking programs such as a course in psycho-synthesis. This new understanding of the nature of a person became an important core component particularly for the seminarians. Also, changes were made through the introduction of pastoral education that is a field-based approach to training missionary priests.

## Era 2: 2008–2011

The narrative data showed too few opportunities to change the culture. The data shows a lack of external support from the Church and the Vincentians. People did not see prospects to change the old into something new. And, sometime they did not see the possibilities of building upon the old pre 2011 culture. By 2011, people believed it was too late for change and something new. The needed changes in the narrative data indicate the necessity for a clear mission statement, funding strategy, updated and better facilities, and new curriculum. There was strong insistence among staff that every degree had to include a number of theology courses. A new curriculum to meet market demands would need new and qualified staff. Such changes demanded new staff that proved to be challenging due to financial constraints. Internal audits, that is, quality assurance and standardized data collecting, were not happening fast enough. There was a need to update the seminary model into a university business model. Even after 30 years, many people still saw the institution as a seminary instead of a university college.

The narrative and survey data, together, showed respondents reported that "others" focus on their own responsibilities and made little or no effort to change internal processes or take actions to change the college's image in the community. There was reluctance to "put ourselves out" in the public arena. People seemed reluctant to move towards more secular programs. Some people seem to believe that a solution will be found which means AHC would continue in its current form.

The documentary data clearly showed the lack of identity within the college coupled with the rapid changes in Church and society along with other external influences. The college was not facing up to the harsh realities in a timely fashion. These multiple factors were slowly leading the college towards its downfall. Both the narrative and documentary data indicate the negative impact the economic recession had during this period. This, along with the lack of financial support from the government and little to no real history of philanthropy, all had negatively contributed to the overall financial health of the college.

During this era, the narrative data comments about the new vision and mission of AHC as a college with a theological dimension rather than a theological college with other dimensions. Participants were still of the opinion that for any vision the relation of the seminary to the Church was necessary. The vision changed when Church conditions changed, that is, the college taught theology with a pastoral dimension. Particular aspects of the value of the programs in AHC should be stressed. During late 2011, under new leadership, there were new planning strategies in place, not least, a new strategic plan called *Aisling 2017* with input from all the staff.

Both the narrative and documentary data of this era indicate a new mission statement was put in place with input from all the staff. Also, there was a new strategic plan, financial plan, and business model drawn up in late 2011, under new leadership.

During this era there was a lot of uncertainty about the future of AHC. Some participants in their narratives were hesitant to move away from offering only theological and pastoral programs and to develop more marketable and secular programs. There was some resistance towards the College offering new "secular" programs. Given the college's program offerings, it was to market, recruit new students, and to make people aware of AHC. There still appeared to be unfounded suspicions about the college from the institutional Church. Finally, information gained from the narratives was that there was untapped potential for the future of the college.

The narrative and survey responses show the college had an ambiguous identity and direction (i.e., "What is the identity of the college and where is it going in the future?"). All Hallows College had an identity crisis up to 2011. The public perception of AHC was that it was still a seminary. It was not seen as relevant in the third level sector. The mission was not reflected internally, there was a lot of talk but the usual barriers to action and change were there (e.g., agreeing the need for change in theory but not in practice).

The narrative and documentary data for 2008–2011 showed identity confusion for the college delayed the required organizational changes to make AHC "fit for purpose." This identity confusion came to the point where financial viability was critical. All Hallows College was used to a precarious financial situation for many years, but in these last years it was coming to a breaking point. Unfortunately, it was too late for the college when changes were made in late 2011 with a new mission statement and a revisionary look at the college's identity to make AHC "fit for purpose and fit for market."

The 2011 new national strategy for higher education (Hunt Report), along with the state of the finances, helped the board of governors realize the urgency for change. The Hunt Report strategies in effect eliminated AHC from the educational market. Both the Hunt Report and finances ignited an urgency to assess and change educational priorities and business practices.

The college documentary data in line with Kotter's Step 2 show the linkage agreement with Dublin City University (DCU) brought forth a needed new model of governance to the college. The linkage agreement brought some consulting resources to the college. The board of governors and a number of key college committees had access to the expertise from colleagues at DCU. The new board of governors (AHC) needed to understand the possible impact of cultural and educational policy shifts and put in place key strategic actions for development.

The narrative and documentary data showed that after many staff meetings comprising of staff from every part of the college coming together, a new AHC Mission Statement was agreed on. Some of the participants in the narrative research were party to developing this new mission statement that helped to identify what AHC was about. The new mission statement has helped in the re-imagined vision for AHC (up to 2014). Many of the participants felt that the timing was wrong or that a lot more time should have been given to turn things around with a new vision and mission.

All Hallows College was founded in 1842. The Vincentian Fathers took over the leadership of the college in 1892. However, the narrative data reports there was not an overly Vincentian ethos in the college until the new mission and vision in 2011. There were still strong emotional ties in 2011 to the seminary and its legacy. Respondents indicated these emotional ties were detrimental for the college to change and move forward. Both the narrative and survey data report there were failures to let go of the past and there was no sense of urgency among staff. Moreover, there were failures to build upon the opportunities to develop into a creditable and relevant third level college, that is, adopt best practices in governance, curricula development, finances, development, infrastructure, and human resource management.

## *Era 3: 2011–2015*

In late 2011, there was new leadership in the College but as with Era 2, 2008–2011, the participants in the narratives continued to comment about their confusion concerning the identity of AHC. During this era, the narrative data comments about the new vision and mission of AHC as a college with a theological dimension rather than a theological college with other dimensions. Participants were still of the opinion that for any vision the relation of the seminary to the Church was necessary. The vision changed when Church conditions changed, that is, the college taught theology with a pastoral dimension. Particular aspects of the value of the programs in AHC should be stressed.

Both the narrative and documentary data of this era indicate a new mission statement was put in place with the input from all the staff. Also, there was a new strategic plan, financial plan, and business model drawn up in 2011. These plans were formalized during Era 3.

Throughout the narratives, participants spoke about their perceptions of what the conditions were in the college which both hindered and helped conditions leading up to organizational changes and the need for a guiding coalition to implement these changes. There was a heightened fear of the unknown and a reluctance to change in the college. People were hesitant to move away from offering only theological and pastoral programs and to develop more marketable and secular programs. Given the college's program offerings, it was to market, recruit new students, and to make people aware of AHC. There still appeared to be unfounded suspicions about the college from the institutional Church. Finally, information gained from the narratives was that there was untapped potential for the future of the college.

During this period, the narrative, documentary, and survey data show a new era of substantial reorganization of structures, administration, programs, and services in the college. The mission of the college was re-imagined leading to promulgating a new mission statement resulting in the new motto "We are here to make a difference." The mission statement led to a new strategic plan, *Aisling* (translated from the Irish—"Vision") *2017: Freedom and Choice in Education*. The plan was undergirded with a specific *Business Sustainability Plan* to properly structure the finances to successfully achieve the strategic goals. The strategic plan created a sense of hope and future vision. There was an increased efficiency of implementation strategy.

According to respondents, the restructuring of the college was an attempt to decentralize authority, operate on the principles of subsidiary and shared governance. The administrative structures were divided into three major divisions: (a) academics, (b) operations, and (c) student life and pastoral care. Moreover, each division was led and supervised by a vice president who reported directly to the president.

The academic structure of the college moved from a three-school model to a one-school model. This was done to strengthen structures, maximize resources, and streamline services. In addition, there was a complete reorganization of academic structures, processes, and procedures. The new Academic Service Unit (a one-stop-shop) brought together into one office the various student services. In addition, a major investment was made to install a new student information system for students' records, to enroll in courses, and to pay student fees. There were new faculty and staff hires to create new programs. In addition, new accountability structures and human resources compliance and procedures were put into place for faculty and staff. There were changes in the curriculum to help the college be more market-friendly and attractive to potential students and increase enrollment (e.g., the innovative program for older adults, Adult Learning BA [ALBA]).

Finally, another major change to the culture of the college was the "resident community" of priests and sisters who taught and worked in the college of years and lived on campus. The residence benefit of these priests and sisters was part of their employment compensation. During this era most of the priests and sisters were part time in the college and/or at some level of retirement. The college had major issues with building safety and code requirements in some of the building occupied by the resident community. In addition, some priests and sisters lived in the college conference center. It was determined that some of the facilities were not "fit for purpose" and posed a health and safety risk to the residence. Also, in order to maximize the resource of the conference center for the needed additional income, the resident community needed to vacate. The resident community found other housing accommodations off campus. They continued to support and work in the college after the transition.

During this period, the narrative, documentary and survey data show a new era of substantial reorganization of structures, administration, programs, and services in the college. The mission of the college was re-imagined leading to promulgating a new mission statement resulting in the new motto, "We are here to make a difference." The mission statement led to a new strategic plan, *Aisling* (translated from the Irish—"Vision") *2017: Freedom and Choice in Education*. The plan was undergirded with a specific *Business Sustainability Plan* to properly structure the finances to successfully achieve the strategic goals. The strategic plan created a sense of hope and future vision. There was an increased efficiency of implementation strategy.

According to respondents, the restructuring of the college was an attempt to decentralize authority, operate on the principles of subsidiary and shared governance. The administrative structures were divided into three major divisions: (a) academics, (b) operations, and (c) student life and pastoral care. Moreover, each division was led and supervised by a vice president who reported directly to the president.

The academic structure of the college moved from a three-school model to a one-school model. This was done to strengthen structures, maximize

**44** ▪ Anchoring Cultural Change and Organizational Change

resources, and streamline services. In addition, there was a complete reorganization of academic structures, processes, and procedures. The new Academic Service Unit (a one-stop-shop) brought together into one office the various student services. In addition, a major investment was made to stall a new student information system for students' records, to enroll in courses, and to pay student fees. There were new faculty and staff hires to create new programs. In addition, new accountability structures and human resources compliance and procedures were put into place for faculty and staff. There were changes in the curriculum to help the college be more market-friendly and attractive to potential students and increase enrollment (e.g., the innovative program for older adults, Adult Learning BA [ALBA]).

Finally, during the era 2011-2015, a major change to the culture of the College occurred. Up to 2011, the "resident community" of priests and sisters who taught in the College over many years were also living on the College campus. The residence benefit of these priests and sisters was part of their employment compensation. During this era most of the priests and sisters were part time in the college and/or at some level of retirement. The college had major issues with building safety and code requirements in some of the building occupied by the resident community. In addition, as some priests and sisters lived in the college conference center, it was determined that some of the facilities were not "fit for purpose" and posed a health and safety risk to the residence. Also, in order to maximize the resource of the conference center for the needed additional income, the resident community needed to vacate. In 2011, the "resident community" found other housing accommodations off campus. They continued to support and work in the college after the transition.

## Conclusion

### Era 1: Pre-1995

During this time

- the *Identity* of AHC was a seminary.
- *Finance* was not a major problem.
- The *Mission* was, "Go teach all nations."
- The Vincentian *Ethos* was very strong.
- 1995–2008–2011 saw changes in the *identity* of AHC from being a seminary to the Institute of Mission and Ministry, which was not totally accepted by all.

- *Finance* was becoming a major issue particularly around 2008 which saw the country in economic crisis. No money was coming from the government.
- The *mission* was, "Go teach all nations." However, as the identity of AHC was changing the mission had to adapt to this new identity.
- The Vincentian *ethos* was very strong.

## Era 2: 2008–2011

- The *mission* was, "Go teach all nations." However as the identity of AHC was changing the mission had to adapt to this new identity.
- The Vincentian *ethos* was very strong.
- From 2008–2011, the mission was, "Go teach all nations." However, the identity of AHC was changing and the mission had to adapt to this new identity.
- *Finance:* Again, finance was becoming a major issue particularly around 2008 which saw the country in economic crisis. Cash reserves were being spent. No money was coming from the government.
- The *mission* was, "Go teach all nations." However, as the identity of AHC was changing the mission had to adapt to this new identity.
- The Vincentian *ethos* was very strong.

## Era 3: 2011–2015

- The *identity* of AHC was changing from an Institute of Mission and Ministry to a third level college linked to DCU.
- *Finance* was at a critical state. As a private college there was very little funding to sustain the college.
- As the identity changed during this era, the *mission* had to adapt to this new identity.
- The Vincentian *ethos* was very strong.

# 5

## *Ethical Leadership and Organizational and Cultural Change*

Since the end of the Second World War in 1945, the world has seen rapid change in almost every aspect of society. The age of technology has provided ways to quickly communicate information worldwide which has challenged, either for good or ill, the way we view ourselves, the world, and social and cultural norms. Many historians, sociologists, anthropologists, and other scholars cite the last 60 years as being a time of greatest change in the history of the world. We have seen tremendous progress in industry, technology, education, science, and medicine. Today, we enjoy a more robust economy and more options for career choices, better access to resources, and greater domestic and international mobility. Of the many consequences of this rapid revolution, people are living longer, changing careers, and migrating to other locations. Although good progress has been made on many fronts in the last 60 years within society, there are obvious losses in values, community, and spirituality that were once held as sacred and unalterable. These changes in society and the loss of such values beckon for new and different kinds of leaders who can navigate the change and growing complexities.

The last decade has been one of crises in leadership within business, banking, Church, and government throughout the world. Society has suffered from the scandals and corruption of leaders who have been placed in positions of trust with fiduciary responsibility to steward resources, serve, and to build up human society. What are the missing elements within these failed leaders? Is it knowledge? Is it skills? How can society prepare a new generation of ethical leaders who are just, service driven, and possess leadership which advocates for the good of all people and the whole of society? What kinds of educational programs are necessary to equip men and women for the formidable challenges of leadership in today's world?

These ponderous questions of leadership are vitally important for the future of our society. Vincentian leadership dedicates its mission to inspire a new generation of women and men to be effective leaders, social entrepreneurs, and innovators contributing to the social, political, and economic advancement of our people. Vincentian (St. Vincent DePaul) values of justice, service, and ethical leadership permeate every decision and action of Vincentian leaders. Justice is the affective value which transforms the human spirit from narcissism to empathy in caring for others. Service is the effective value which enables people with the skills, competencies, professionalism, motivation, and courage to respond to the real needs and problems of people, communities, and society. Finally, leadership is the advocacy value which empowers people to work and give voice for systemic change on behalf of others who are poor and who have no voice.

In Vincentian Family (2010) we are told that St. Vincent DePaul (1581–1660) was a dynamic and charismatic leader with an ability to form unique relationships, coalitions, alliances, and organizations that addressed the great social needs of his time. The uniqueness of these relationships was found in his ability to bring together and work with widely diverse groups of people. Real change occurs when people are organized, educated, supported, and equipped to be advocates and social change agents for those most in need. Like Vincent DePaul, Vincentian leaders today reach out and invite people into service, build networks, and provide the needed education, skills, and support systems in the mission to liberate and alleviate the miseries of other people. This mission continues to challenge leadership to be authentic in reaching out to the international, national, and local social issues of our times.

The Vincentian approach to leadership is person-centered and pragmatic which helps people discover and find their power to be self-sufficient, knowledgeable, skilled, and advocates for social justice to improve the quality of life for all people. The goals of Vincentian leadership aim toward integration and mastery of professional skills in research, theory, and community practice. Vincentian mission, vision, and values beckon an approach to leadership that are relevant, realistic, holistic, and fully integrated within human and community experiences. Schön (1983) asserts that true human service and leadership professionals need to do more than just perform actions; they need the skills for reflection-in-action for integration. To accomplish the necessary integration of research, theory, and practice for future leaders, Vincentian leaders endeavor to provide innovative methodologies and community-based experience to guide the ascertainment of knowledge and skills for future leaders.

The Vincentian mission and the Vincentian approach to leadership first ask the question, "What must be done?" And, specifically, what must be done for people and communities who are in the greatest of need? Therefore, Vincentian leaders seek out and commit to ambiguous and daunting missions which are often considered by other people as impossible. Vincentian leaders approach the impossible with faith and assurance in divine Providence (which means God will support and guide the mission) and with a commitment to work hard in a spirit of creativity and innovation. This ethos is realized through building personal and community relationships. This is where Vincentian leaders build relationships and respond to the mission. It is critical for the Vincentian mission that leaders align themselves and work collaboratively with business, government, nonprofit, and faith-based organizations. Together these four sectors work together to address both the immediate needs of people as well as working toward systemic change to transform the systems and structures which keeps people in poverty (Vincentian Family, 2010).

In 2016, narrative research was carried out in All Hallows College (AHC). One of the aims was to look at the influence of ethical leadership and its relationship to organizational change and cultural change. From the results regarding perceptions of leadership style, it seems that this is a very important, if not the most important, factor in any organizational change and indeed cultural change. Our research was analyzed under Kotter's steps. The following data collectively examines three eras of AHC (Pre-1995–2008; 2008–2011; 2011–2015).

> *Step 1: Establishing a Sense of Urgency.* Help others see the need for change and they will be convinced of the importance of acting immediately.

*Step 2: Creating the Guiding Coalition.* Assemble a group with enough power to lead the change effort and encourage the group to work as a team.

*Step 3: Developing a Change Vision.* Create a vision to help direct the change effort and develop strategies for achieving that vision.

The data from the case study carried out at AHC examined the factors of leadership style and organizational change. The results from the case study were incorporated into Kotter's steps as outlined above.

## Leadership Style and Organizational Change (Incorporating Kotter's Steps 1–3)

### Pre 1995–2008

From the narratives, it was perceived that pre 1995 (1980s/1990s) the leadership style was imaginative and visionary. It was also thought pre 1995 that the president as leader realized the old culture needed urgent change.

In 1987, three members of AHC Staff spent 3 months in Munich carrying out a needs analysis among Irish people. Based on the results, recommendations were made to the Irish Bishops Conference who asked AHC to take responsibility for setting up and monitoring the running of the Irish mission.

### 1995–2008

There was a need for inspirational leadership to change from seminary to lay ministry. There was also a need for leadership to adapt to changes in the needs of the Church.

The impetus for change was from Fr. Jim McCormack CM (who came to AHC from studying in Louvain) and Fr. Bob Whiteside (who came to AHC from studying in Notre Dame, United States). New programs and educational resources were introduced.

Under new leadership in 1995, research was carried out by means of consultation with Dublin diocesan priests about the feasibility of running a Preparing for Lay Ministry program and introducing new BA degree programs and Research MA and Taught MA Programs. This came about because the seminary model had to change to make the college "fit for purpose" and also because tensions were caused by people not wishing to change from a seminary to an institution of mission and ministry.

New leadership in 1995 continued to manage the vision of Kevin Rafferty in developing programs to promote the mission and ministry particularly of school leavers, mature students, and international students. Strategies developed during this time included: (a) formulating a statement of All Hallows Direction and Priorities (2000), (b) formulating formal and structured policy documents on Data Protection College Policy and Guidelines (2007) and College Web Site Policy Document (2007), (c) setting up a counseling service for students in 2006, (d) setting up an MA program in management: community and voluntary services (2006), (e) the opening of the John Hand Library in 2006, (f) All Hallows College Adult Learning Feasibility Report (Nov. 2006), (g) capital campaign 2006–2010 operational plan which set out a strategic plan for fundraising and finance, (h) restructuring the BA program (April 2008), (i) ministry with integrity-ethical guidelines for staff and students (Sept. 2008), All Hallows College Records Management Policy (2008), (j) the most important strategy at this time was the agreement for institutional linkage between AHC and Dublin City University (DCU) which, although drafted in 2007, came into being in 2008.

From 1995–2008 the leadership was about maintaining the status quo. There were a lot of unfinished organizational and cultural changes during this era. Management rather than leadership was perceived. During that era, there was a need for a strategic change to accompany a curriculum change and the profile of the students but there did not seem to be a great urgent need for change.

The continuation of managing an institution developed from a seminary rather than a third level college of education linked to a university was in evidence. During this era, the Irish Vincentian provincial was very supportive of the endeavors of the college.

Also during this era, leadership consisting of a pastoral approach to education was in place. This contributed to over-functioning staff and under-functioning students. There was no formal HR department.

In responding to the possibility of assembling a group with enough power to lead any change effort, it was thought, although with some opposition, that the president up to 1995 had great vision and change and was able to bring a team with him to guide the necessary changes. The president from 1995 onwards inherited financial burdens and this proved more difficult, though not impossible, to bring in innovative courses relating to the ethos and to bring in new programs and methods.

Leadership and management at AHC, towards the year 2008, found itself with a dilemma. How could the seminary model survive the changes in both the Church and society? How could it be sustainable in a world without sufficient on-going funding? All Hallows College had succeeded in generating some short wins. Although the ethos stayed the same throughout, it had to make very big organizational changes using a business model, which used change structures and policies that may not necessarily have fitted the vision.

The staff involved with the emerging changes were not rewarded to any degree. It was still viewed that the work at AHC was vocational in nature rather than career oriented. The financial director was still referred to as the "Bursar."

The main opposition in encouraging a group to work as a team was the ambiguous identity of direction of the college. On the other hand, from the narratives, there was encouragement for collaboration. Other positive points were made which were sources of collaboration in leading change. They included: (a) a financial stability feeling; (b) support and fundraising of past-men; (c) change of curriculum, differentiating the institution from before; (d) in relation to governance, it is concluded that there were unfinished changes from seminary to college; (e) there was operational management in existence rather than strategic leadership; but (f) the introduction of pastoral education for the formation of seminarians was seen as a major step forward.

## *2008–2011*

In the second era, management rather than leadership continued to be perceived. During that era, there was a need for a strategic change to accompany a curriculum change and the profile of the students. There appeared to be a lot of unfinished changes both organizationally and culturally. But the cultural change needed a leader rather than a manager to develop an institution from a seminary culture to a third level college of education linked to a university. The leadership style affected change because of a need for collaborative leadership [up to 2011]. There was also the need for stronger leadership to go into the future. There was a great need to streamline middle management positions.

From 2008–2011 there were three more new programs in the process of being introduced to AHC. These new programs together with staff who had been made redundant in another institution came to work in AHC bringing a different culture with them. As these new programs and staff were not fully incorporated into the AHC culture, this led somewhat to disunity and a barrier to team building and group work.

At this time in the college also, governors and trustees were unknown to staff. One major problem seemed to be the disconnectedness between trustees and management staff regarding direction and focus of college programs and activities. Attitudes towards leadership were mixed as some thought that leaders did not understand problems or making changes fast enough. Some staff thought that the ability of trustees/management could successfully find solutions from some whereas there was a degree of denial from others. Up to late 2011, it was thought that leaders were very cautious about initiatives. Some of the other perceptions about the leadership (2008–2011) include the "leaders" were "talking the talk" but not "walking the walk" which allowed staff to demonstrate energy around discussion of the proposed new leadership and accepting accompanying changes. However, in some cases some pretended to accept the changes but there was very little evidence of this acceptance. Also, those with little or no leadership responsibilities expressed lack of communication and lack of decisiveness on the part of those at the top, and those at the top express lack of communication and efforts towards change on the part of those with less management responsibility. There was no willingness to remove unqualified leaders and there were ineffective lines of reporting and accountability.

The president of the college inherited many financial burdens. At the same time new programs and methods and staff were introduced and there was little encouragement to work as a team. From the narratives also, there did not seem to be appropriate leadership to further linkage to the university and sustainability. The major dilemma was that of finance—without adequate finance there could be no sustainability of the programs and staff members.

During this era a new strategic plan needed a leader for future viability of staff and finance. There was a need to influence and respond to issues outside the college. A new mission was needed and strategic partnerships were needed to be developed.

1. The "linkage agreement" between AHC and DCU was in essence a great opportunity for a group to lead the change effort and encourage the group to work as a team. Unfortunately for AHC, this put pressure on an already overworked staff. The agreement could be management to a certain extent but there was little or no qualified leadership to oversee the huge changes that were taking place. All Hallows College needed more staff to keep up with the demands of DCU but there was no money to do so. Any power to lead the change effort was among 2 or 3 individuals.
2. Because of the Irish financial crash which began around 2008, AHC lost financially both from the reduction of the many sources of income including the rental of offices and income from the conference centre. As a privately funded college without government funding it became impossible to sustain the financial level necessary to keep going.

3. In David Tuohy's document *All Hallows Strategic Plan Phase 2: Developing Priorities-Focus on Action* (July 2010), he suggested that a key alliance for AHC is that with DCU. He suggested that the college needed to be well informed on developments in DCU who were in the process of restructuring their own alliances. He also suggested setting up meetings with other "linked" colleges to discuss the implications of developments in DCU. He said that AHC should ensure support and good communication strategy arising from meetings in DCU. A stronger alliance was essential between AHC and the diocese. David Tuohy also urged to seek ways of giving incentives in time and other rewards to staff involved in program development and administration. As well, it is important to clarify the executive role and responsibilities of officers and committees within the college.
4. A group of people from the staff got together and worked on producing new policy documents including the *Code of Conduct, Ministry With Integrity, Records Management Policy, Data Protection, Child and Vulnerable Adult Protection Policy,* etc. (All updated 2012–2013). In order to write these policy documents, the staff members had to work as a team.
5. The *All Hallows College Research Report 2010* was led by a staff member who had enough power to lead change but there was opposition and it was difficult to encourage a team effort.
6. David Tuohy recommended that a team effort was needed to review the cost effectiveness of different programs and activities in the college according to agreed protocols. It was also necessary to develop a set of guidelines for reflecting on the result of such costing, balancing the mission values and the business requirements, and stating how individual programs may be linked to the whole. The role and responsibility of the board of governors must be developed and promoted. There is a clear need to focus on its leadership role and focus on policy and strategy for the college. The trustees are committed to a process of influence rather than a controlling relationship with the board of governors.
7. In assigning areas for review, 4 key sets of actors are needed to work together as a team with strong leadership involved:
    – *The Trustees*: (a) refining the mission of AHC, (b) positioning the conference and retreat center, (c) arranging alliances and partnerships, and (d) ensuring financial viability.
    – *{BSL}Board of Governors*: The four issues above and (e) management structures and partnerships, and (f) finance, marketing, promotion, and fundraising.

- *Academic Council:* (a) undergraduate programs, post-graduate programs, research, school for adult and community education taken as a unit; (b) structures; and (c) support structures.
- *Staff:* (a) undergraduate programs, (b) post-graduate programs and research, (c) school for adult and community education, and (d) support activities.

## 2011–2015

However, in late 2011, when the new president was appointed, he articulated the connections between the new behaviors and organization success, and developed the means to ensure leadership development and succession. His style of leadership—collaborative leadership—was "new" to AHC. He motivated and encouraged leadership as much as possible. He was conscious of succession. He introduced the *Aisling 2017 Plan* which was a major strategic plan for the changing culture of the college from seminary to institute to a third level college within a university while keeping the Vincentian ethos of ethical leadership, social justice, and service. A member of staff suggested the name for this strategic plan—"*Aisling*"—which epitomizes the changing culture at AHC.

In this era of post-2011, from our research, many of the respondents were of the opinion that the leadership was imaginative, visionary, and collaborative. He had a different organizational vision and strategy influenced by the United States experience and using the United States model to change from an institution of mission and ministry to a 3rd level business world in the context of the Vincentian ethos. This posed its own difficulties in that the change in the Irish Vincentian provincial had dramatic consequences for the college, as the Irish Vincentian province were withdrawing from education, and specifically AHC as a place of learning. Other difficulties occurred, for example, (a) resistance to the new leadership role; (b) adapting to a United States business approach model; (c) one participant's perception was that in introducing new leadership in 2011 the distance between management and staff increased, but other respondents did not find this to be so from their experience; (d) good communication about organizational changes could have improved the situation.

The president of the college during 2011–2015, as part of his leadership, set up the following:

1. *Aisling 2017 Strategic Plan/Executive Summary/New Mission Statement.* The staff was called together over several staff meetings in order to write a "new" mission statement. The new mission statement is:

> All Hallows College is a Catholic & Vincentian higher education institution. All Hallows educates women & men to be effective leaders engaged in justice and service championing social & educational participation. The college is committed to excellence in teaching research & professional development. All Hallows is a College of Dublin City University. We are a welcoming, diverse, student-centered international community of learning. (All Hallows College Mission statement 2011)

The staff were also made aware of the urgency of repositioning the college and asked to help with writing and incorporating a new strategic plan named "*Aisling* (the Irish word for dream) 2017": A Strategic Plan 2013–2017.

2. The president also set up a *Business Sustainability Plan 2013–2017*. This business sustainability plan 2013–2017 has at its core the *Forfás Report 2013* which states:

> Social enterprise is a small but growing part of the enterprise base and ecosystem that has potential to bring further job gains and deliver economic potential. There is both a demonstrated need and a market for, social enterprise in Ireland. With the appropriate enabling and promotional effort, there appears to be scope for increasing jobs in the sector. (Forfas Report, 2013, p. 2)

All Hallows College, its executive summary focuses on two main areas: academics and conferencing and guest services. Major adjustments were: (a) salary reduction adjustments for all staff and (b) replacement of religious staff with lay staff. In line with the objectives of the *Aisling* Strategic Plan 2017, the president with a management team devised a center of excellence in leadership and human services in collaboration and partnership with other bodies.

In 2014 the All Hallows College management team selected by the president consisted of the deputy president, executive vice presidents, the director of finance, the dean of academic affairs, and the academic council.

## Conclusion

Several conclusions were drawn regarding leadership and organizational change.

Up to 2011, there was an absence of strategic leadership and strategic organization.

In 2011, there was a move for strategic leadership but it was in a different culture and during a storm of external changes.

Historically, there has been an underdeveloped governance process and structure. When the governance process and structure came about it was in response to external *not* internal pressures.

There was an absence of both strategic and operational competency up to recent years. During two eras, (1995–2008, 2008–2011), it was perceived that it was Formation in Theology rather than Theological Education.

There was a need for different styles of leadership during the three eras. The leadership styles determined organizational and cultural change.

# 6

# Social Justice and Organizational and Cultural Change

One of the core values of Vincentian tradition is that of social justice, the others being ethical leadership and service.

1. Justice is the affective value which transforms the human spirit from narcissism to empathy in caring for others.
2. Ethical leadership is the advocacy value which enables people to work for and give voice to systematic change on behalf of others who have no voice.
3. Service is the effective value which equips people with the skills and competencies, professionalism, motivation, and courage to respond to the real needs and problems of individuals, communities, and society at large.

Vincentian policies are based on the formula that

social justice + advocacy + systematic change = freedom, peace, and progress

In the article, "Vincentian Leadership: Advocating Social Justice," Craig B. Mousin (2005) writes:

> Understanding justice:
>
>> Although Saint Vincent, Saint Louise, and Frederick Ozanam were committed to justice, we find little to define justice in their writings. Certainly they knew justice, or perhaps more accurately, they knew injustice and sought to relieve that wherever found. Today, to be an advocate for justice in a Vincentian legacy, we first need to seek an understanding of justice which enables all in this great community to work toward justice in our dealings with each other. (pp. 245–246)

Mousin continues

> William Hartenbach, C. M., reminds us "the classic definition of 'justice' is fidelity to the obligations of one's relationships" ... justice is giving to each person what is due to him or her. Tis certainly echoes the traditional western understanding of justice, *suum cuique*—giving to each what is due has influenced philosophers and theologians from the Greeks to the Romans, Roman Catholics and Protestants. Among the cardinal virtues, justice ranks highest based on its orientation towards others. Without justice in relationships decisions become based solely on power, or simply "small-minded wealth-or–interest maximizers, incapable of fruitful participation in the common good." (p. 255)

The Vincentian philosophy and approach to social justice is not necessarily unique to Vincentians. As illustrated in the quotes of the following three famous people:

> Life's most persistent and urgent question is, "What are you doing for others?" (Martin Luther King, 1957)
>
> Where justice is denied, where poverty is enforced, where ignorance prevails, and where any one class is made to feel that society is an organized conspiracy to oppress, rob, and degrade them, neither persons nor property will be safe. (Frederick Douglas, 1886)
>
> Whatever community organization, whether it's a women's organization, or fighting for racial justice ... you will get satisfaction out of doing something to give back to the community that you never get in any other way. (Ruth Bader Ginsburg, 2017)

However, Vincentians see social justice through the lenses of their relationship with Jesus Christ and his mission to bring good news to the poor. The Vincentian tradition of social justice embodies a spirituality that love of neighbor is the same love one has for Christ (Mark 12:28–31; John 13:34–35;

Luke 10:25–37). This spirituality is evident in the 268 institutes that make up the "Vincentian Family" (https://cmglobal.org/en/vincentian-family/).

Advocacy is an essential value and a core element of social justice in the Vincentian tradition. Vincentian advocacy must include both working "with" and "alongside" the poor, as well as working "on behalf" of the poor. These two aspects of advocacy manifest the spiritual truth that we effectively serve others only in love and in relationship with them as brothers and sisters.

Vincentian social justice and advocacy had a 122-year tradition at All Hallows College (AHC). In recent years, the values of social justice and advocacy were most evidently embodied in two AHC programs: (a) adult learning Bachelor of Arts (ALBA) and community-based service learning (cbsl). The ALBA program was modeled on DePaul University's competency-base curriculum designed for older returning students to third level education. The competency-based approach afforded older students who at one time saw higher education as not an option due to financial or academic circumstances. ALBA enabled students to receive academic credit for achieving learning competencies acquired in their past life and work/professional experiences. This facilitated incoming students with some level of achievement and confidence as they began their higher education goals and pursuits. For older students, beginning ALBA with acknowledged achievements provided an attitudinal disposition for "success" rather than being in a position of "deficit." Lastly, the advocacy and support for ALBA was also found in the fee structure of the program. In order to attract older students who were economically unable to pursue higher education, student fees were considerably lower than the standard college fees. Several religious communities in Ireland offered financial support to supplement the difference.

Community-based service learning or sometimes referred to as "pastoral experience" had a long tradition at AHC. Even before this educational concept of community-based learning became popular and a standard aspect to third level education, AHC made cbsl a regular part of its curriculum since the 1960s. The AHC's cbsl program gave students real life experiences in working within the community addressing people's personal and social issues. The skills for social justice and advocacy were developed in both the experiences as well as the personal and group reflections of those experiences. The reflections were directed, connected, and integrated to the discovery and learning that students found in their academic readings, research, and classroom lectures and discussions. The unique Vincentian values of advocacy and social justice were made tangible in the growing awareness, empathy, and compassion of students.

The tools of advocacy in Vincentian social justice include systemic change of programs to empower and advocate for historically oppressed and disadvantaged populations—also, to remove barriers and overcome social injustice and address achievement and access gaps. Ultimately, Vincentian social justice and advocacy is about the radical and spiritual transformation of the whole world.

In our research, the Vincentian core value of social justice manifested itself throughout and in particular when analyzed under Steps 1–3 of Kotter's (2012) Eight Step Process "Leading Change."

*Step 1: Establishing a Sense of Urgency.* Help others see the need for change and they will be convinced of the importance of acting immediately.
*Step 2: Creating the Guiding Coalition.* Assemble a group with enough power to lead the change effort and encourage the group to work as a team.
*Step 3: Developing a Change Vision.* Create a vision to help direct the change effort and develop strategies for achieving that vision.

## Social Justice, Organizational and Cultural Change

### *1980–Pre 1995*

Social justice 1980–Pre 1995: In 1980 when AHC was a seminary there was a change in direction with the introduction of the psycho-synthesis understanding of the nature of the person, and includes the spiritual dimension. The second major change was the introduction of pastoral education for the formation of the seminarians to help them in their missionary work in a changing Church and society. Sr. Moya Curran OP was instrumental in introducing these changes.

Fr. Kevin Rafferty saw the urgent need for change from the seminary to lay involvement in the Institute of Mission and Ministry. A document which provided this need for change was the *Curran Report* (1983) which the terms of reference for Fr. Curran's research was "to investigate and evaluate the formation for ministry at AHC in relation to the needs of the Church today, the developing concept of ministry, and the traditional mission of AHC to go, teach all nations" (p. 1).

The data from the case study carried out at AHC examined the factors of social justice and organizational and cultural change. The results from the case study were incorporated into Kotter's (2012) eight step process "leading change."

## 1995–2008

Under new leadership in 1995, research was carried out by means of consultation with Dublin diocesan priests about the feasibility of running a Preparing for Lay Ministry program and introducing new BA degree programs and Research MA and Taught MA Programs. A specific program of study was set up on the concept of social justice during this era. New leadership in 1995 continued to manage the vision of Kevin Rafferty in developing programs to promote the mission and ministry, particularly of school leavers, mature students, and international students.

Strategies developed during this time included: (a) formulating a statement of All Hallows Direction and Priorities (2000); (b) formulating formal and structured policy documents on (i) Data Protection College Policy and Guidelines (2007) and (ii) College Web Site Policy Document (2007); (c) setting up a counseling service for students in 2006; (d) setting up an MA program in management: community and voluntary services (2006); (e) the opening of the John Hand Library in 2006; (f) All Hallows College Adult Learning Feasibility Report (Nov. 2006); (g) Capital Campaign 2006–2010 Operational Plan (All Hallows College, 2008) which set out a strategic plan for fund-raising and finance; (h) restructuring the BA program (April 2008); (i) Ministry With Integrity: Ethical Guidelines for Staff and Students (Sept. 2008) and All Hallows College Records Management Policy (2008). The most important strategy at this time was the agreement for institutional linkage between AHC and Dublin City University which, although drafted in 2007, came into being in 2008.

On February 14, 2002, the statement of All Hallows Direction and Priorities (2000) and all the documents above were communicated to all staff members, mainly in committee meetings and the academic council at AHC. In this document, social justice is seen as one of the main priorities of AHC. All Hallows College (2000) is a learning community committed to the mission of Jesus Christ and to the development of people for ministry. The priorities are

- to be a community of education in theology and related disciplines.
- to offer formation and support for pastoral leadership and promote the development of collaborative ministry.
- to be a community to prayer and worship.
- to work for justice with particular attention to the poor and powerless.
- to foster an environment of hospitality and welcome.
- to promote an environment of hospitality and welcome.
- to promote imaginative responses to the searching of young people in their faith journey (p. 2).

## 2008–2011

In 2009, the introduction of the new program adult learning BA degree (ALBA) was part of a vision for the college which was adapting the college to the needs of a changing society and Church but keeping the ethos of AHC.

In 2010, in David Tuohy's *Strategic Plan for All Hallows College,* a number of tensions were identified with regards to the vision and the mission statement. In the current context of third level review and economic downturn, there is a question of the survival and viability of the college. A key tension is between the survival of the mission and the survival of the institution. It is a question of focus and instrumentality. Is the college an instrument of the mission? Or is the mission an instrument of the college? These two positions are not mutually exclusive, but the balance achieved between them has implications for resource allocation and perhaps more importantly for the expectations on staff. The action needed?: To revisit the mission and vision statement with the different stakeholders with the view of re-stating them. The aim would be, through the process and the product, to give an energized focus to the work of the college.

In 2010, Tuohy makes the following points in his document. There is a strong sense of affirmation that developments in the college over the past 5 to 10 years reflect the original mission [and vision] of the college, faithfully responding to changing circumstances. As such, AHC faithfully responds to a call for mission and ministry. The belief is that AHC had made and continues to make, a major contribution to empowering individuals and groups in society through promoting a reflective dialogue between their faith and their cultural/work experience. These reflections contain a strong focus on (a) the content of the programs and (b) the process balancing academic rigor and professional pastoral experience and where the target audience with those involved in Church, the not-for-profit, and the voluntary sector. He suggests that obstacles can be overcome by (a) removing Church-based language, (b) getting a clear understanding of ministry, (c) considering the global demands and standards for judging third-level institutions, and (d) realizing the competition for physical space on the campus.

## 2011–2015

All Hallows College identifies from its core values, in particular ethical leadership, social justice and service, and existing academic strengths leadership and human services as its distinctive institutional activity and academic specialization. Consistent with an historical development of the college's provision and educational practice from the foundational disciplines of applied theology and pastoral care, the college has over the years diversified and established a number of innovative awards and research themes, some of which are unique in Ireland, that enables its academic strategy to coalesce today around the specialization of leadership and human service. Human services, as a unifying discipline, is intrinsically linked to the professional competencies of leadership and management within the increasingly specialized field of human service activities in the nonprofit, voluntary, community, pastoral, health, custodial, and statutory care sector. Academically, it advances a transferable holistic model of human service knowledge, skills, and values that address human needs through an interdisciplinary knowledge base—focusing on the prevention and solution of problems, enhancing the dignity and empowerment of people, and improving the overall quality of life of individuals and communities served. Vocationally, in addition to meeting the traditional formative objectives of higher education, it meets the increasing demand for highly specialized professional skills and roles within the human services sector, embracing, complementing, and enhancing, and in some cases, replacing, existing state services.

In May 2013 the following minutes were discussed at the board of governors meeting, reflecting the future vision for the college stressing the postgraduate programs in a Level 9 taught Postgraduate Professional Frame: Leadership and Human Services:

> Disciplines include (1) leadership, (2) non-profit management, (3) pastoral care, (4) psychology, (5) applied Christian spirituality, (6) ecology, (7) ethics, (8) community development, (9) cross-professional supervision, (10) theology and religious studies, (11) social justice, (12) economics, (13) public policy, (14) counseling and accompaniment, (15) social entrepreneurship, and (16) adult education.

In 2013, the major vision at AHC during the era 2011–2015 was the conception and development of *Aisling 2017*.

## Aisling 2017 Strategic Plan/Executive Summary/New Mission Statement

When launching the new strategic plan *Aisling 2017*, the president wrote:

> As a community of learning, we welcome diversity and hold that our core motivating values of social justice, service, and leadership can be shared by people from all traditions and cultures. Our vision is a new generation of values-centered social entrepreneurs and innovators contributing to the advancement of all people. But as St Vincent De Paul says: "It is not enough to do good. It must be done well." (Hay Leadership Project)

The vision to help direct the change effort was the *Aisling 2017 Strategic Plan*, divided into 9 areas. Within each of these areas were strategic initiatives, objectives, and specific actions, approximately 546 in total. The *Business Sustainability Plan 2013–2017* was also part of the vision to help direct the change effort. According to the Forfás Report 2013, the nonprofit sector in Ireland employs upwards of 100,000 people and generates revenue of over 6 billion euro. Within this, the smaller but emergent social enterprise sector employs between 25,000–33,000 people in a diverse range of over 1,400 social enterprises generating an income of approximately 1.4 billion euro.

In 2014, the president wrote in his blog:

> The goals of AHC's leadership education aim toward integration and mastery of professional skills in research, theory, and community practice. Our mission, vision, and values summon us to develop programs that are relevant, holistic, and fully integrated within human and community experiences. Schön (1983) asserts that true human service and leadership professionals need to do more than just perform actions; they need the skills for reflection-in-action for integration. To accomplish the necessary integration of research, theory, and practice for future leaders, All Hallows endeavors to prove innovative teaching and learning methodologies and community-based experience to guide the ascertainment of knowledge and skills for future leaders. (Schon, 1983, p. 354)

## Conclusion

The main conclusion from this data is that throughout the three eras researched, the unique Vincentian values of advocacy and social justice were made tangible in the growing awareness, empathy, and compassion of students, from seminarians to third level college students.

# 7

# *Internal and External Challenges and Organizational and Cultural Change*

Every organic entity constantly faces internal and external challenges for change and growth. If an organic entity remains stagnant, it will surely demise without hope of new life and growth. However, if the organic entity engages the challenges and is open for change and greater growth, death will bring new life and possibilities. Throughout its 172 years tradition, All Hallows College (AHC) faced many internal and external challenges such as the crises of the Irish famine, poverty, oppression, and many cultural and political changes. Throughout all these challenges, AHC remained focused on its mission to respond to the needs of the times. The mission was a focal point for people to rally around and to stand united in the struggle. Most recently in its history, AHC responded proactively to the racial changes of the Church's Second Vatican Council reforms. In fact, compared to other seminary programs, AHC was progressive with implementing the necessary changes to prepare students for the new reality. In the 1980s, AHC responded to the challenge of declining enrollments by opening the college programs to non-seminary students.

The ongoing transformation of AHC from a seminary to a religious pastoral training college to a liberal arts college continued throughout the 1990s and 2000s. Although AHC made some significant changes in the 1980s and 1990s in response to the growing internal and external challenges and changes, the college never really let go of its seminary identity even though seminarians had not been enrolled since the early 1990s. The rapid economic, curricular and political changes to the international higher education landscape in the 2000s were not fully studied and addressed by the college. For example, in the early 2000s, AHC aligned itself with Dublin City University (DCU) and DCU became the degree granting institute for AHC. Although strategically this was a beneficial move for AHC's future, the college did not fully address the greater infrastructure issues of finances, fundraising, political feasibility, curriculum, and staffing to grow and sustain AHC as a viable, contributing, and sustaining institution serving Ireland, Europe, and the international community. In many ways, the DCU connection became a life line for short-term survival instead of an opportunity to expand, serve, and develop the mission and vision for the needs of the time and for market feasibility. Historically, the college's infrastructure was frail and insufficient. The college had very few to no political allies and did not have the financial capital to build a real and vibrant future. In many ways, contrary to its mission and early legacy, the college as an academic institution did not take the leadership role and facing the horrible and destructive clergy sex abuse scandal, the realities of the rapid changes in higher education, and economic and market realities.

Metaphorically, AHC chose to grow comfortable with its legacy behind the large walls surrounding its campus and its narrow gate entrance on Grace Park Road. To a great degree, AHC viewed the internal and external threats and cultural changes as hazards and not the opportunities they were for building a future. The college became accustomed to react and respond to problems instead of opening itself to the risk of real possibilities to continue its mission and legacy into the future.

However, in the latter part of 2011 with new leadership, many positive changes began to take place in the college. Alas, it seemed that they came too late in a rapidly changing environment. In our narrative research, we looked at the internal and external challenges, organizational change, and cultural change incorporating Steps 1–3 of Kotter's Eight Step Process "Leading Change" (2012):

> *Step 1: Establishing a Sense of Urgency.* Help others see the need for change and they will be convinced of the importance of acting immediately.

*Step 2: Creating the Guiding Coalition.* Assemble a group with enough power to lead the change effort and encourage the group to work as a team.

*Step 3: Developing a Change Vision.* Create a vision to help direct the change effort and develop strategies for achieving that vision.

The data from the case study carried out at AHC examined the factors of internal and external challenges, organizational change, and cultural change. The results from the case study were incorporated into Kotter's steps as outlined above.

## Internal and External Challenges, Organizational Change, and Cultural Change

### *Pre 1995–2008*

In order to see the need for change and for acting immediately, it is important to realize what the internal challenges and the external challenges are. It is also important to determine sources of complacency, that is, reluctance or otherwise to act immediately to overcome these challenges.

The major external challenges recognized by the narratives was the experience of main changes taking place in the environment at the time, that is, the changes taking place both in the Church and in society. In the post 1979 Irish Church there was a fall in vocations. Unfortunately, there was also an unsupportive attitude towards AHC from the institutional Church.

The main internal challenge consisted of the Vincentian ethos not evidenced overtly up to 2011. In relation to governance, the perception was that there were unfinished changes from seminary to college. Also there was operational management rather than strategic leadership/management. The emotional connections to seminary model were blocks leading to little or no change in a timely manner. Also, there was a need for the structure of the curriculum to change in order to make the college fit for purpose. The main source of complacency perceived from the narratives in this era included the tensions caused by people *not* wishing the college to change from the seminary to an institution.

In responding to the possibility of assembling a group with enough power to lead the change effort, it was thought, although with some opposition, that the president up to 1995 had great vision and change and was able to bring a team with him to guide the necessary changes. The president from 1995 onwards, inherited financial burdens and this proved more difficult though not impossible to bring in innovative courses relating to the ethos and also to bring in new programs and methods.

The main opposition in encouraging a group to work as a team was the ambiguous identity of direction of the college. On the other hand, from the narratives encouragement for collaboration, three positive points were made which were sources of collaboration in leading change. They were: (a) a financial feeling of stability, (b) support and fundraising of past-men, and (c) change of curriculum, differentiating the institution from before.

**Mission and Vision**

From the Narratives, the focus of the mission was on lay formation and adult education. It was also about broadening higher education—particularly education with a theological dimension, and also being unique in providing pastoral placements within the programs. The mission and the vision were dependent on support from the institutional Church.

**Vision Strategy**

There appeared to be a lack of clarity shared about re-imagining the vision (i.e., changing from seminary to institute to college.

## *2008–2011*

During this period of transition where AHC became a linked college to a university, the participants in their narratives were aware of external challenges, mainly from the changes taking place in the higher educational policy and landscape in Ireland. Also, this was at the beginning of a major recession in Ireland after years of the "Celtic Tiger" where spending above our means had been the order of the day. The investments that AHC made for the future were hit very much. During this era, there was no visible support from the government, particularly financially. Although AHC became a "linked" college with the university, there was no one suitably qualified or able to lead the college into the next phase of education at AHC. During this era also, there seemed to be a breakdown in communication and relationships about the "new" status of AHC. In addition, a major factor was the external challenge of post 1979 where there was a dramatic fall in vocations which in turn affected the student cohort.

In relation to internal challenges, from the narratives, the Vincentian ethos was not followed or in evidence overtly up to the time of the new leadership in the latter part of 2011. There were unfinished changes from the seminary model to a business model in the governance of the college.

There were still emotional connections to the seminary model, which may have proved detrimental in blocking any necessary organizational change.

Information from the narratives included the perception that there was operational management rather than strategic leadership/management. The funding strategy was not strong enough to ensure future viability. Around this time also, there was an influx of new programs and new staff from other institutions which had been wound down. Some of the "new" staff saw the college as an opportunity to continue as they had before rather than adjusting to the ethos of the college.

During this era, some of the sources of complacency included not being able to "let go" of the seminary to the institution to the college, and not sensing the urgency of having to change to become a third level university college. There was a failure to build on opportunities; there was little or no understanding of best practice management (HR procedures). Some of the main sources of complacency were poor timely communication, a pre-supposed support of the value of the AHC vision, and the internal focus of reality.

From the narratives there did not seem to be appropriate leadership to further linkage to the university and sustainability. As stated before, the major dilemma was that of finance—without adequate finance there could be no sustainability of the programs and staff members.

Throughout the narratives, participants spoke about their perceptions of what the responses were to conditions in the college which both hindered and helped conditions leading up to organizational changes and the need for a guiding coalition to implement these changes. The responses were that there seemed to be an ambiguous identity and direction, that is, "What is the identity of the college and where is it going in the future?" There still appeared to be unfounded suspicions about the college from the institutional Church. Information gained from the narratives was that there seemed to be untapped potential.

Other responses included the issue of "free fees" from the government, there was an undercurrent of mistrust from disenchanted minority, in particular from the "new" staff. Tensions between administration and academic staff manifested and there appeared to be an absence of focus to enable change. Again, during this era, a main challenge was that of finance. From the narratives, some of the participants thought that the research program expanded regardless of the college financial position leading to a disproportionate budgeting of programs.

More positively, from the narratives, some of the participants lauded the wonderful support and fundraising of past-men. The change of curriculum, and differentiating the institution was very positive as was the use of limited resources. The changes from the "Hunt Report" (Hunt, 2010), that is, the change in the higher education environment where it was recommended that small colleges/institutions merge with larger bodies, was seen as positive rather than negative.

When commenting about the vision and mission of AHC, the following idea emerged—that AHC was a college with a theological dimension rather than a theological college with other dimensions. Participants were of the opinion that for any vision the relation of the seminary to the Church was necessary. The vision changed when Church conditions changed, that is, the college taught theology with a pastoral dimension. A final comment from the participants was that particular aspects of the value of the programs at AHC should be stressed.

From the narratives, when commenting about the vision strategy, participants mentioned that there was a lack of clarity about re-imagining the vision strategy in organizational change, that is, change from institute of lay ministry to college. Also, from the information, there seemed that there was some opposition to build broader supportive relationships.

## 2011–2015

In September 2011, a new president was appointed to the college, a Vincentian from DePaul University in Chicago. He saw the need for urgent changes to take place at AHC and set about convincing all about the importance of acting immediately in order to survive as a college. In the narratives, it can be seen that there indeed was an awareness especially among the staff of the college for the need of urgent organizational change but, as before, they realized that there were several challenges and a sense of complacency to be overcome before making these necessary changes.

From the narratives, participants stated that the external challenges included external stakeholders as both society and the Church was changing rapidly and Ireland was at the height of an economic recession. There was no support from the government, financially or otherwise.

There was a limited linkage agreement with the university who were at the initial stages of putting the recommendations from the government document, the Hunt Report (Hunt, 2010; "National Strategy for Higher Education to 2030") into reality. During this era there was change in Irish higher education policy and landscape. There was no place for small colleges, particularly faith-based colleges in Ireland.

At this time there seemed to be a breakdown in communication and relationships between the college and external stakeholders. Some of the perceptions in the narratives were that there was no support from the Irish Vincentian province and the "secular" Church. One of the major points raised was that there was no history of educational philanthropy in Ireland (as per the United States model).

Other external challenges to be met were (a) the need for change in the institutional Church to have a more supportive role with the college, (b) the new BA program—adult learning BA (ALBA)—was initially sponsored by religious orders and others, but there was a need for finance to ensure sustainability; and (c) the college status within the Irish educational system had to be re-defined.

Internally, the participants in their narratives suggested that there was a need for a re-visioned funding strategy. It was also suggested that the structure of the curriculum needed to be changed.

Up to this era, the majority of the staff was priests/religious sisters who saw their work as a vocation rather than a profession and worked for stipends. When more qualified lay staff were employed (due to the growth of new programs and a new type of students) and paid a salary, tensions surfaced. In addition, during this era the changes in staffing proved to be an internal challenge. In another narrative, a participant was of the opinion that in internal operations reality checks were not happening in time.

Major sources of complacency from the information in the narratives were the pre-supposed support of value of AHC vision. Another source of complacency perceived was that in the form of not facing up to financial reality in a timely fashion. There was a certain amount of complacency in the changes from seminary to institution and possibly the organizational changes needed in changing from an institution to a third level college was not considered as urgently as it should have been. One of the causes may have been poor timely communication.

From the narratives relating to this era (2011–2015) there was encouragement for collaboration and three positive points were made which were sources of collaboration in leading change. They were: (a) a financial feeling of stability, (b) support and fundraising of past-men, and (c) change of curriculum, differentiating the institution from before.

**Finances as Challenge**
The president of the college inherited many financial burdens. At the same time, new programs and methods and staff were introduced and there was little encouragement to work as a team. The major dilemma was that of

finance—without adequate finance there could be no sustainability of the programs and staff members.

Throughout the narratives, participants spoke about their perceptions of what were the responses to conditions in the college which both hindered and helped conditions leading up to organizational changes and the need for a guiding a coalition to implement these changes. The responses were that there seemed to be an ambiguous identity and direction, that is, "What is the identity of the college and where is it going in the future?" There still appeared to be unfounded suspicions about the college from the institutional Church. Information gained from the narratives was that there seemed to be untapped potential.

Other responses included the issue of "free fees" from the government; there was an undercurrent of mistrust from disenchanted minority, in particular from the "new" staff that were not fully incorporated into the AHC culture. Tensions between administration and academic staff manifested and there appeared to be an absence of focus to enable change. Again, during this era, a main challenge was that of finance. From the narratives, some of the participants thought that the research program expanded regardless of the college financial position leading to a disproportionate budgeting of programs.

More positively, from the narratives, some of the participants lauded the wonderful support and fundraising of past-men. The change of curriculum and differentiating the institution was very positive as was the use of limited resources. The changes from the "Hunt Report" (Hunt, 2010), that is, the change in the higher education environment where it was recommended that small colleges/institutions should merge with larger bodies, was seen as positive rather than negative.

From the narratives, many of the participants were very positive about new changes brought about by the new president in 2011: (a) they spoke about the innovative courses relating to the ethos, new programs, and methods; (b) the operation of new structures; (c) a new director of finance appointed in the college was seen as positive; (d) some spoke of an improved dialogue between the college and the archbishop of Dublin; (e) there was a realization for the urgent need of management systems; (f) human resource management was put on a formal legal structure as was (g) quality promotion.

There were new planning strategies in place, not least, a new Strategic Plan *Aisling 2017* with input from all the staff. A new mission statement was put in place from the input of all the staff. A new financial plan was drawn up in 2011. A new business model of operations was also put in place during this era. A completely new strategic leadership structure took place with a senior management team put in place. There was also a change in the membership and roles and responsibilities in the board of governors and academic council in the college. Roles and responsibilities were identified. A stable environment for students was also initiated during this era. Organizationally, changing from a seminary to a business model resulted in the residential community no longer lived on campus.

With any kind of change, particularly organizational change, comes opposition. The major perceptions from the participants in their narratives about which of the factors were responsible for hindering change, included: (a) tensions between administration and academic staff, (b) the critical financial situation, (c) the research program expanding without due consideration of the college's financial position, (d) the Irish Vincentians pulling out of education, (e) lack of commitment to change due to internal suspicions about changes and inadequate communication of the *Aisling 2017* Plan, (f) the lack of support for sustainable change to last, (g) a mismatch between programs and support system, (h) the perceived growth of secularism in society negating the need for any kind of faith-based education, and (i) the perception, particularly in 2014/2015, that without proper financial support there is no possibility of sustainability.

When commenting on possible positive helpful responses to the conditions, the participants suggested that changes in the curriculum helped to differentiate the institution, the changes in the higher education environment when looked at in a positive light helped the college to adapt. In the year 2014/2015, during the beginning of the wind-down of the college, a positive response was the realization of the financial situation leading to an agreed cut in salaries. Also, it was commented by one of the participants that there was excellent effective communication in the wind-down, and a sense of fairness throughout the procedures.

## Conclusion

### *Pre 1995–2008*

- There was a need for more community-based programs.
- Make theology/spirituality have a broader base and relevant to both Church and society.
- All Hallows College's ethos and good reputation need to continue.

## 2008–2011

- After many staff meetings comprising of staff from every part of the college coming together, a new AHC mission statement was agreed on.
- The new mission statement has helped in the re-imagined vision for AHC (up to 2014).
- Many of the participants felt that the timing was wrong or that a lot more time should have been given to turn things around with a new vision and mission.
- Vincentian ethos was not followed overtly until 2011.
- Emotional connections to the seminary model may have been detrimental to change—failing to build on opportunities to change to a third level college.
- No understanding of best practice human resource management.
- Failure to let go—there was no sense of urgency among some staff.

## 2011–2015

The vision of AHC from 2011–present was based on (a) particular aspects of the value of programs and (b) the Vincentian ethos post 2011 was very much influenced by the United States Vincentians. The vision was also changed because of the redefinition of the role of AHC as a provider of third level education (2011).

From their narratives, some participants were of the opinion that there seemed to be opposition to build broader supportive relationships. Again, some felt that the issue appears to be the change approach needed to adhere to the vision. Many of the participants felt that the timing was wrong or that a lot more time should have been given to turn things around with a new vision and mission.

# 8

## Conclusions and Recommendations

The state of higher education in the United States and Europe are facing massive challenges given the projected decline in the number of 18 year olds available for enrollment, the rapid changes in the job market, and the needed education programs to respond to such demands. The economy of higher education today requires specialized infrastructure and amenities both for training purposes and attracting suitable students. The competition for getting students for one's institution has made the higher education landscape a buyers' market for students. Many colleges and universities have dropped required entrance exams and other traditional requirements of the past in order to admit and enroll students.

This growing competition is particularly challenging to smaller, private, and faith-based institutions that more often than not have little to no government funding, smaller endowments, and are operationally tuition dependent. In contrast to the past, religious students and families today are less likely to choose a college or university solely based on the institutions' religious affiliation, values, or mission. Today, religious students and families, similar to their nonreligious counterparts, are making choices about higher education based more upon cost, brevity of time it takes to complete their degrees, and getting the needed knowledge and skills base for employment. This change in the market and economy of higher education has tested the traditional notions of the liberal arts approach found in religious affiliated institutions. This approach is one of leisure and learning for the sake of learning, providing for students a well-rounded learning experience. The ultimate goal for faith-based schools is to form good, faith-filled, and mature citizens prepared for both life and career. Our research for the book was in the form of a case study. The case study set out to answer the following research question.

**Research Question:** *Why is anchoring cultural change an important component of organizational change?*

In order to achieve answers, our aim and objectives were as follows.

### Aim of Research

To examine the relationship between cultural change and organizational change at All Hallows College (AHC), Dublin over 20 years (1995–2015).

### Objectives

1. To illustrate the factors (both positive and negative) influencing cultural change (e.g., *identity, finance, mission and ethos*) of AHC.
2. To illustrate the *Vincentian social justice* value influencing cultural change.
3. To evaluate the role of *leadership* in cultural and organizational change.
4. To determine the *external and internal challenges* to cultural change at AHC.

Following an analysis of data received from narrative, quantitative, and documentary research in relation to AHC, Dublin 1995–2015 using John Kotter's *Eight Step Process for Leading Change* (see Appendix 6), several major conclusions were drawn.

### Conclusions

1. These changing times are points of reflection for faith-based higher education institutions to re-examine their mission, vision, values,

and strategy in the student market place. Similar to publicly funded institutions, religious schools have the same ethical and moral obligations to prepare their students at the highest level of education standards in order that they can be competitive and employable.
2. Moreover, faith-based sponsored institutions have a unique opportunity to provide additive value to students' higher education experiences. That is to say, the faith-based mission goes beyond the humanistic institutional values of secular and government funded and sponsored schools. The mission of such institutions are deeply rooted in many centuries of liberal arts education tradition (education that provides freedom and liberation) and espouses the sanctity of the human person as a mirror image of the divine Creator. The mission commitment is to love and care for students and their well-being and development. Other long held traditions of faith-based institutions include commitments to social responsibility and justice, advocacy for marginalized people, and community service. And, in turn, students will bring this mission, values, and learning into the world. The ultimate end result of any faith-based mission is *transformation* of the individual, the community, and the world. The challenge for faith-based schools is how to embody, package, and sell their mission to a growing secular society.
3. The learning from AHC is fourfold: (a) to be clear and embolden the mission, vision, and values; (b) to listen to the signs of the times and the need of the education and employment market; (c) to constantly stay in line with all aspects of infrastructure: economic, curricular, facilities, communication, research, faculty, and external supporters; and (d) develop political friends and allies to help companion the mission and cause of the institution.
4. The All Hallows story, along with the data and analysis presented in this study, demonstrates the need for colleges and universities to be nimble and able to adopt change in serving their education mission, while remaining a relevant and vital force within society.
5. Although All Hallows made many changes over the years, the college was unsuccessful in both adopting and anchoring a culture of change and progress and ascertaining supports and resources to remain sustainable and germane to the education needs of society. The eventual change in the college was implemented with fear and caution and failed to involve broader strategic thinking and greater wide-ranging changes.
6. Furthermore, the evidence shows that changes from a seminary, to an institute of mission and ministry, and to a liberal arts college brought a sense of "mission drift" or "mission confusion." After the seminary and the institute of mission and ministry, it was very dif-

ficult for people to talk about the college's purpose and its unique niche. Instead, the college had become "a bit of everything" and included a number of different religious charisms. It was not until 2011 that college clearly marked its mission and ethos along the Vincentian charism.

7. In November 2011, Fr. Dennis Holtschneider, the then president of DePaul University in Chicago advised the All Hallows' leadership to begin reframing our leadership strategy from "survival" to "serving the mission." According to Holtschneider, the survival approach is about reacting to and against crises. Such an approach leaves a trail of confusion and exhaustion, whereas the mission approach breeds a sense of focus, faithfulness, opportunities, possibilities, and progress.

> The Holtschneider meeting began a radical paradigm shift for the leadership direction of the college. Soon after, the leadership inaugurated a process to renew the college's mission, vision, values, and strategic direction. This simple change from "survival" to "mission" brought renewed hope and energy to the college. Moreover, serving the college mission brought clarity to direction and decisions about the future. Although, in the end, it was decided that All Hallows needed to end its operation and close as a college. The clarity and ability to make this difficult decision came out of standards and obligation of mission and values-based institution. In moving forward, the mission question was asked: "What is in the best interest of the students, staff, faculty and community"?

8. The All Hallows 2011–2015 era revealed the needed connection between "mission development" and "leadership." Leadership is essential for mission development and a mission culture. Successively, leadership finds its grounding and direction from the mission.

9. The All Hallows project demonstrates the need for higher education to develop capable leaders who understand the culture and the nature of change to successfully lead from the standpoint of mission and progress. Historically, higher education has promoted leaders with years of academic success without real leadership and experience in mission and business. It is essential as never before that college and university leaders have an in-depth knowledge of mission development, change strategies, leadership skills, and successful business models.

10. The overall conclusion gleaned from our study is that anchoring cultural change is an important (if not the most important) component of organizational change because it forms the core for *transformation* of the individual, the community, and the world, which in turn is the ultimate end result of any faith-based organization.

## *Recommendations*

All Hallows College served the Catholic Church, Ireland, the international community, and higher education for 172 years. The college leaves behind an amazing legacy of education grounded in mission, values, and a vision of social justice, care, and compassion. Likewise, the college offers lessons for today's institutions about the importance of mission development and focus, value-centered leadership, care for persons and the importance of maintaining every aspect of the schools' infrastructures. Colleges and universities of the future need to be bold and courageous in responding to the economic and social needs of society.

The concluding words of this study is one of gratitude to the countless men and women who have worked, studied, supported, and contributed in any way to the great life and mission of AHC. It was truly a unique and special institution that gave so much good to individuals, communities, and the world. For those of us who were privileged to share part of 172 years of the All Hallows journey, may we be enabled to pass on to others some of the good we have received and experienced. May we hold true to the college's motto, "Euntes Docete Omnes Gentes"—"Go and Teach All Nations."

# Narrative Research

## *Sampling, Guideline for Questions, and Analysis Among 20 Participants*

The first part of the research consists of obtaining narratives and analyzing them. When designing the Narrative research in this study, Jane Elliott (2007) in her book provided us with practical guidelines of how to use narrative research qualitatively. The narratives are basically the participant's experience at All Hallows College (AHC), specifically in relation to perceived/actual organizational changes and responses.

Twenty key actors, for example, from both academic and administrative cohorts who have worked at AHC gave their narratives for analysis in the research, some by written narrative, others by interview. Guidelines for questions were used.

1. Pre 1995–2008
2. 2008–2011
3. 2011–2015

*Note:* Some of the participants have worked in overlapping eras.

## Sampling Narrative Interviews: Purposive Sampling

### *Purposive Sampling*

John Dudovskiy (2018), in his e-book, *The Ultimate Guide to Writing a Dissertation in Business Studies: A Step-by-Step Assistance,* writes in Chapter 4 that *purposive sampling* (also known as judgment, selective, or subjective sampling) is a sampling technique in which the researcher relies on his or her own judgment when choosing members of population to participate in the study.

Purposive sampling is a non-probability sampling method and it occurs when "elements selected for the sample are chosen by the judgment of the researcher. Researchers often believe that they can obtain a representative sample by using a sound judgment, which will result in saving time and money" (Dudovskiy, 2018, Chapter 4). Alternatively, purposive sampling method may prove to be effective when only limited numbers of people can serve as primary data sources due to the nature of research design and aims and objectives.

In purposive sampling, personal judgment needs to be used to choose cases that help answer research questions or achieve research objectives. Dudovskiy (2018) continues:

### *Advantages of Purposive Sampling (Judgment Sampling)*

1. Purposive sampling is one of the most cost-effective and time-effective sampling methods available.
2. Purposive sampling may be the only appropriate method available if there are only a limited number of primary data sources who can contribute to the study.
3. This sampling technique can be effective in exploring anthropological situations where the discovery of meaning can benefit from an intuitive approach.

### *Disadvantages of Purposive Sampling (Judgment Sampling)*

1. vulnerability to errors in judgment by researcher,
2. low level of reliability and high levels of bias, and
3. inability to generalize research findings.

Purposive sampling was used for the narrative research in the case study. The main reason for using this type of sampling here was that there was only a limited number of primary data sources which could contribute to the study. A further complication was that some of the actors worked at AHC over more than one of the eras in the research.

In order to be as objective as possible, some members of the case study team who had joined the AHC staff over the past few years interviewed some of the staff members from the past eras as they did not know them. Also, the guide questions for the narratives used were based on John Kotter's (2012) Eight Step Process for Leading Change—helping objectivity.

## Guidelines for Completing Narrative Case Study Research Evaluation Project All Hallows College, February 2015

All of the guiding questions relate to your experience in AHC during any or all of the following periods: 1995–2008, 2008–2011, and 2011–2015.

### *Guidelines for Completion of Your Narrative*

**K.1:** *What do you think were the urgent challenges faced by AHC internally and externally?*

What are your reflections regarding sources of complacency for organizational change at AHC?

**K.2:** *Who responded to these conditions and how?*

What helped or hindered the effectiveness of these responses?

**K.3:** *What has been your experience of the vision and mission of AHC?*

In your experience, how effective was the AHC strategy in achieving its vision and mission?

What are your reasons for this?

**K.4:** *Who and how were the vision and mission of AHC communicated?*

How were peoples' concerns and anxieties addressed?

**K.5:** *From your experience, what helped organizational change in AHC?*

From your experience, what hindered organizational change in AHC?

What role did leadership in AHC play in organizational change?

In your experience was there resistance to organizational change?

If so, how was it manifested and responded to?

**K.6:** *In your experience what kind of organizational changes in AHC were successful?*

**K.7:** *In your experience, were successful organizational changes in AHC continually built on?*

**K.8:** *From Kotter's research, there is a relationship between organizational change and the culture of the organization. The following is a quote from Kotter (2012) which may help you answer the questions that follow it:*

> "Culture" (corporate) refers to the "norms of behavior" and "shared values" among a group of people in an organization. "Norms of behavior" are common or pervasive ways of acting that are found in a group and persist because group members tend to behave in ways that teach these practices to new members, rewarding those who fit in and sanctioning those who do not. "Shared values" are important concerns and goals shared by most of the people in a group that tend to shape group behavior and that often persist over time when group membership changes. (p. 156)

In your experience did the attempts at organizational change at AHC seek to build on or to replace the established culture at AHC? Can you describe some examples?

In your experience what organizational changes were developed in the culture of AHC?

Any other comments or reflections?

Thank you very much for your cooperation in helping with this research. All information is for research purposes only.

APPENDIX B

*Quantitative Survey (Questionnaire/Survey Monkey)*

Sampling, Questionnaire, and
Analysis of Survey of 63 Alumni Respondents.

The second part of the Rresearch consists of an analysis of a Survey Monkey among alumni over the past 20 years.

## Sampling Quantitative Survey

A Survey Monkey was sent to a stratified random sample of alumni over the last 20 years. Because of the difficulty of not having email addresses from alumni previous to 2008, a stratified sample was made by post to alumni from 1995–2008 and a sample selected from email addresses from 2008 onwards. The stratified random sample consisted of sampling 4 respondents from each year among all the undergraduate and postgraduate programs a total sample of 80 respondents of which 63 respondents replied.

## Sampling: Stratified Random Sample

Stratified random sampling is defined as: A population sample that requires the population to be divided into smaller groups called 'strata.' Random samples can be taken from each strata or group. Stratified random sample is a probabilistic sampling option and each strata is mutually exclusive.

The main advantage of stratified random sampling rather than simple random sampling is that it is used when the categories of the strata are thought to be too distinct and too important to the research interest. A stratified random sample promotes great precision and often requires a smaller sample.

A disadvantage of stratified random sampling is that researchers must identify every member of a population being studied and classify them into one and only one subpopulation.

Alan Bryman (2012) suggests that the steps in a stratified random sample are as follows:

(a) The starting point is to categorize the population into "strata" (relevant divisions),
(b) so the sample can be proportionately representative of each stratum,
(c) then, randomly select within each category for a simple random sample (Chapter 8).

**Sample:** 63 Alumni were sampled (see Table B.1). The sample involved several of the respondents who would have studied at All Hallows College over the three eras (Table B.2).

**TABLE B.1 Sample of Alumni Who Responded**

|  | $N$ |
|---|---|
| Survey Monkey Returned | 56 |
| Postal Questionnaires Returned | 7 |
| Total | 63 |

**TABLE B.2 Respondents in Each Era**

|  | $N$ |
|---|---|
| 3 Eras (Pre 1995–2008, 2008–2011, 2011–2015) | 23 |
| 2 Eras (2008–2011, 2011–2015) | 19 |
| 1 Era (2011–2015) | 21 |
| Total | 63 |

## Questionnaire: A Copy of the Survey Monkey and Paper Questionnaire

All the guiding questions relate to your experience at AHC during any or all of the following periods: 1995–2008, 2008–2011, and 2011–2015.

*Please circle or tick all that apply.*

**Social Profile Details:**

Q.1(a) Gender     Male 1     Female 2

Q.1(b) Age Range
- ☐ 18–23 years
- ☐ 24–29 years
- ☐ 30–39 years
- ☐ 40–49 years
- ☐ 50–59 years
- ☐ 60–69 years
- ☐ 70+ years

Q.1(c) Status: When you first came to AHC, how would you describe your status?

☐ Laity     ☐ Religious (Non-ordained)     ☐ Ordained

Q.1(d) Program of Studies:
- ☐ Undergraduate
- ☐ Postgraduate
- ☐ Pathways
- ☐ RFM
- ☐ Other please specify _____

Q.1(e) When did you start in All Hallows College?
_____

Q.2 K1(a) From your experience as a student in AHC what 2 organizational changes would you have made?
_____
_____
_____
_____
_____

K.1(b) From your experience as a student in AHC, what do you think was the biggest challenge facing AHC?

_____
_____
_____
_____

Q.2 K.2 From your experience as a student in AHC, who had the greatest influence in the running of the college?

_____
_____
_____
_____

Q.3 K.3(a) When you were a student at AHC, what were the vision and mission of the College?

**Vision**

_____
_____
_____
_____

Mission

_____
_____
_____
_____

K.3(bi) In your view, did these need to change?

Yes 1     No 2     Don't Know/Unsure 3

K.3(bii) Please elaborate on your answer to K.3(bi)

_____

_____

_____

_____


K.4(ai) In your experience as a student in AHC in relation to the effective communication of the vision and mission, which of the following apply? In the table below are suggested key elements in the effective communication of the vision in an organization change process. Please tick/circle the level of agreement with the following:

| | Communication of the vision and mission of AHC was effective because of | | | |
|---|---|---|---|---|
| 4 | Simplicity | Yes 1 | No 2 | Unsure 3 |
| 5 | Use of a Metaphor/Analogy | Yes 1 | No 2 | Unsure 3 |
| 6 | Multiple forums (e.g., meetings) | Yes 1 | No 2 | Unsure 3 |
| 7 | Formal/informal interaction | Yes 1 | No 2 | Unsure 3 |
| 8 | Repetition | Yes 1 | No 2 | Unsure 3 |
| 9 | Leadership by Example | Yes 1 | No 2 | Unsure 3 |
| 10 | Give and Take (2-way Communication) | Yes 1 | No 2 | Unsure 3 |

K.5(ai) Did you feel valued as a student at AHC?

    Yes 1    No 2    Unsure/ Sometimes 3

K.5(aii) If "Yes" to K.5(ai) In what ways?

_____

_____

_____

_____


K.5(b) As a student, did you have the opportunity to contribute your views regarding change in the college?

    Yes 1    No 2

Q.6 K.6 In your experience as a student in AHC, what 2 organizational changes were successful?

_____
_____
_____
_____

Q.7 K.7(ai) As a student, were you encouraged to contribute to the continuous improvement of the college?

Yes 1    No 2    Unsure 3

K.7(aii) Please elaborate on your answer to K.7(ai)

_____
_____
_____
_____

Q.8 K.8 Why did you choose to study at AHC? Please give 2 reasons.

_____
_____
_____
_____
_____
_____

Any other comments or reflections?

_____
_____
_____
_____

*Thank you very much for your cooperation in helping with this research. All information is for research purposes only.*

# Quantitative Survey (Questionnaire/Survey Monkey)

*Sampling, Questionnaire, and Analysis of Survey of 37 Staff/Stakeholders*

The third part of the research consists of an analysis of a survey monkey among 37 staff/stakeholders who would have worked/been associated with All Hallows College over the past 20 years spanning three eras.

## Sampling Quantitative Survey

A Survey Monkey was sent to a stratified random sample of staff/stakeholders over the last 20 years. Because of the small numbers and easy identification of respondents involved, the following are conclusions drawn from the responses of this cohort of people across the three eras, which reflects their general perceptions, attitudes, and experience giving an overall picture of their association as students/alumni of All Hallows College.

The stratified random sample consisted of sampling 2 respondents from each year among all the undergraduate and postgraduate programs a total sample of 40 respondents of which 37 respondents replied.

## Sampling: Stratified Random Sample

Stratified random sampling is defined as: A population sample that requires the population to be divided into smaller groups called "strata." Random samples can be taken from each strata or group. Stratified random sample is a probabilistic sampling option and each strata is mutually exclusive.

The main advantage of stratified random sampling rather than simple random sampling is that it is used when the categories of the strata are thought to be too distinct and too important to the research interest. A stratified random sample promotes great precision and often requires a smaller sample.

A disadvantage of stratified random sampling is that researchers must identify every member of a population being studied and classify them into one and only one subpopulation. Alan Bryman (2012) suggests that the steps in a stratified random sample are as follows:

The starting point is to categorize population into "strata" (relevant divisions), so the sample can be proportionately representative of each stratum, then, randomly select within each category a simple random sample.

**Sample:** 37 Staff/Stakeholders were sampled (Table C.1). The sample involved several of the respondents who would have been staff/stakeholders at All Hallows College over the three eras (Table C.2).

**TABLE C.1  Sample of Alumni Who Responded**

|  | N |
|---|---|
| Survey Monkey Returned | 34 |
| Postal Questionnaires Returned | 3 |
| Total | 37 |

**TABLE C.2  Respondents in Each Era**

|  | N |
|---|---|
| No information | 6 |
| 3 Eras (Pre 1995–2008, 2008–2011, 2011–2015) | 13 |
| 2 Eras (2008–2011, 2011–2015) | 2 |
| 1 Era (2011–2015) | 16 |
| Total | 37 |

## Questionnaire: *A Copy of the Survey Monkey and Paper Questionnaire Among 37 Respondents Comprising of Staff/Stakeholders*

**Questionnaire for Case Study Research Evaluation Project**
**All Hallows College, February 2015.**

All the questions relate to your experience at AHC during any or all of the following periods: 1995–2008, 2008–2011, and 2011–2015.

Social Profile Details:

(a) Gender    Male 1    Female 2

(b) Period at AHC _____

(c) Major Role at AHC _____

(d) Major Responsibility _____

(e) If staff, were you ever a student at AHC?    Yes 1    No 2

If Yes, What dates? _____

When you first came to AHC how would you describe your status?

Laity 1    Religious (Non-Ordained) 2    Ordained 3

K1 and K2:

(a) From your experience, what were the 2 urgent challenges faced by All Hallows College internally?

_____
_____
_____
_____
_____
_____
_____

(b) From your experience, what were the 2 urgent challenges faced by All Hallows College externally?

_____
_____
_____

(ci) On reflection, what sources of complacency for organizational change in AHC did you observe?

Please elaborate on your answer to (ci)

K.3(a) Please describe your understanding of the Vision of All Hallows College?

K.3(b) Please describe your understanding of the mission of All Hallows College?

Appendix C: Quantitative Survey ■ 99

K.3(c) Please describe your understanding of the strategy of All Hallows College to achieve this mission?

_____
_____
_____
_____

K.3(d) Please rate the AHC strategy to achieve this mission:

    Very Good 1    Good 2    Neutral 3    Fair 4
    Not Good 5    Don't Know 6    Not applicable 9

K.4(a) In your experience, was your understanding of the AHC strategy effectively facilitated by the following?

| | | | |
|---|---|---|---|
| Its Simplicity: | Yes 1 | No 2 | Unsure 3 |
| Use of a Metaphor/Analogy: | Yes 1 | No 2 | Unsure 3 |
| Multiple forums (e.g., meetings, formal/informal interaction): | Yes 1 | No 2 | Unsure 3 |
| Repetition: | Yes 1 | No 2 | Unsure 3 |
| Leadership by Example: | Yes 1 | No 2 | Unsure 3 |
| Give and Take (2-way Communication): | Yes 1 | No 2 | Unsure 3 |

K.4(bi) Were peoples' anxieties and concerns addressed?

    Yes 1    No 2    Unsure 3

K.4(bii) If "Yes" to 4(bi) How?

_____
_____
_____
_____

K.5(a) From your experience, please list 2 factors which helped organizational change in AHC?

_____

_____

_____

_____

K.5(b) From your experience, please list 2 factors which hindered/prevented organizational change in AHC?

_____

_____

_____

_____

_____

K.5(c) Please rank the following from 1–6 (1 being the most important) in empowering people to effect organizational change in AHC:

_____ Communicate a sensible vision to employees ____

_____ Make structures compatible with the vision ___

_____ Provide the training employees need ____

_____ Align information and personnel systems to the vision

_____ Confront employees who undercut needed change

_____ Other (please specify) _____

K.6 Generating Short-Term Wins (Positive Changes)

*Please circle the level of agreement in the following statements:*

Strongly Agree  1      Agree  2      Neutral/DK  3
Disagree  4      Strongly Disagree  5      Not Applicable  9

**The role of short-term positive changes in AHC:**

| | |
|---|---|
| Greatly helped to justify the short-term costs involved | 1 2 3 4 5 9 |
| After a lot of hard work, positive feedback builds morale and motivation | 1 2 3 4 5 9 |

| | |
|---|---|
| Gives the guiding coalition concrete data on the viability of their ideas | 1 2 3 4 5 9 |
| Clear improvements in performance makes it difficult for people to block needed change | 1 2 3 4 5 9 |
| Provides evidence for those higher in the hierarchy that the transformation is on track | 1 2 3 4 5 9 |
| Turns neutrals into supporters, reluctant supporters into active helpers | 1 2 3 4 5 9 |

K.7 Please circle your level of agreement with the following statements:

Strongly Agree 1     Agree 2     Neutral/DK 3
Disagree 4     Strongly Disagree 5     Not Applicable 9

| | |
|---|---|
| Over the last 20 years at AHC, more rather than less organizational changes were needed | 1 2 3 4 5 9 |
| Additional people should be brought in, promoted, and developed to help with all the changes | 1 2 3 4 5 9 |
| Leadership should come from senior management | 1 2 3 4 5 9 |
| Lower ranks in the hierarchy should both provide leadership and manage project changes | 1 2 3 4 5 9 |
| In order to make changes easier both in the short and long term, managers at AHC should identify unnecessary interdependencies and eliminate them | 1 2 3 4 5 9 |

K.8 Kotter's (2012) research saw a relationship between culture and organizational change.

> "Culture" (corporate) refers to the "norms of behavior" and "shared values" among a group of people in an organization. Norms of behavior are common or pervasive ways of acting that are found in a group and persist because group members tend to behave in ways that teach these practices to new members, rewarding those who fit in and sanctioning those who do not. Shared values are important concerns and goals shared by most of the people in a group that tend to shape group behavior and that often persist over time when group membership changes. (p. 156)

K.8(ai) In your experience, did attempts at organizational change and the introduction of new practices at AHC

    Build on established culture     1

    Replace the established culture    2

    Both                                       3

K.8(aii) Please elaborate on your answer to K.8(ai)

_____
_____
_____
_____

K.8(b) Please circle your level of agreement with the following statements:

Strongly Agree 1     Agree 2     Neutral/DK 3
Disagree 4     Strongly Disagree 5     Not Applicable 9

**Culture (corporate) is powerful because:**

| | |
|---|---|
| Individuals are selected and indoctrinated so well | 1 2 3 4 5 9 |
| The culture exerts itself through the actions of the majority of people | 1 2 3 4 5 9 |
| All of this happens without much conscious intent and thus is difficult to challenge or even discuss | 1 2 3 4 5 9 |

Any other comments/reflections/observations?

_____
_____
_____
_____
_____
_____
_____

*Thank you very much for your cooperation in helping with this research. All Information is for research purposes only.*

APPENDIX D

## Documentary Research

*Sampling, Documents Researched, and Analysis of 23 Documents*

The stratified random sample consisted of sampling 23 Documents—3 from Pre 1995–2008, 8 from 2008–2011, and 12 from 2011–2015.

### Sampling: Stratified Random Sample

Stratified random sampling is defined as: A population sample that requires the population to be divided into smaller groups called "strata." Random samples can be taken from each strata or group. Stratified random sample is a probabilistic sampling option and each strata is mutually exclusive.

The main advantage of stratified random sampling rather than simple random sampling is that it is used when the categories of the strata are thought to be too distinct and too important to the research interest. A stratified random sample promotes great precision and often requires a smaller sample.

A disadvantage of stratified random sampling is that researchers must identify every member of a population being studied and classify them into one and only one subpopulation.

Alan Bryman (2012) suggests that the steps in a stratified random sample are as follows:

- the starting point is to categorize population into "strata" (relevant divisions),
- so the sample can be proportionately representative of each stratum,
- then, randomly select within each category a simple random sample.

## Documentary Research Documents Used

### Pre 1995–2008

Sample of documents where organizational change impacted AHC:

1. Directions and Priorities (Mission Statement) 2000.
2. Draft Copy of the Linkage College Agreement with DCU 2007–2008.
3. Summary Report of Academic Council (AHC) to Board of Governors 2008.

### 2008–2011

Sample of documents where organizational change impacted AHC:

1. Narrative Data Traditional Culture, Seminary Legacy 2008–2011.
2. Agreement for Institutional Linkage Between All Hallows College and Dublin City University, February 2008.
3. Minutes of the Board of Directors Meeting, June 2009
4. Strategic Plan 2010–2015, June 16, 2009
5. Policy Documents Board of Directors, September 2009
6. Research Activity Development 2009–2014 and All Hallows College Research Report 2010
7. Strategic Plan Exploratory Stage, June 2010 (David Tuohy)
8. Developing Strategic Objectives, March 3, 2011 (Board of Governors/David Tuohy).

## 2011–2015

Sample of documents where organizational change impacted AHC:

1. *Aisling 2017* Strategic Plan/Executive Summary/New Mission Statement
2. Business Sustainability Plan 2013–2017
3. Fund-Raising Planning October 2013
4. Reorganization Plan October 2011
5. All Hallows BOG Discussion on the "Hunt Report" (National Strategy for Higher Education to 2030) 2011/2012
6. Towards a Future Higher Education Landscape 2012
7. Musings From President 5/19/2013
8. Letter From Minister of Education and Skills Re: Possible Funding From Higher Education Authority (HEA) for AHC 2013
9. President's Blog 2014
10. Sample of Minutes From Board of Governors (BOG) 2012/2013/2014
11. Sample of Minutes From Quality Promotion Committee 2013/2014
12. President's Report to the Past Men of AHC, July 2014.

# APPENDIX E

# *Case Study Research Evaluation*

## Research Methodology

Yin cites Schramm's (1971) definition of the "case study" as a research method. The essence of a case study, the central tendency among all types of case study, is that it tries to illuminate a decision or set of decisions: why they were taken, how they were implemented, and with what result (Yin, 2014, p. 15).

Yin (2014) develops this further by offering a two-fold definition. The first deals with the scope of the study and the second with the relevant features of the case study.

1. The scope of a case study: A case study is an empirical inquiry that
   - investigates a contemporary phenomenon ("the case") in depth and within its real-world context, especially when
   - the boundaries between phenomenon and context may not be clearly evident.

2. The features of a case study: A case study enquiry
   - copes with the technically distinctive situation in which there will be many more variables of interest than data points and as one result
   - relies on multiple sources of evidence, with data needing to converge in a triangulating fashion, and as another result
   - benefits from the prior development of theoretical propositions to guide data collection and analysis.

## The Uses of Case Study Research in Evaluations

There are three types of uses of case study research in evaluations:

1. case study research as part of a larger evaluation;
2. case study research as the primary evaluation method:
   a. focus on the initiative,
   b. focus on outcomes, and
   c. focus on initiatives and outcomes.
3. case study research as part of dual-level evaluation arrangements.

Two good examples of case study research are: T. Bradshaw in 2007 and P. Mayo in 2008. Bradshaw looks at a Community and Mayo looks at a military base. For the purpose of the case study research at AHC, the case study research as the primary evaluation method is preferred, with the focus on initiatives and outcomes. Yin (2012, pp. 49–165) supplies us with examples of 21 applications of a case study. These case studies include (a) Descriptive case studies, (b) Explanatory case Studies, (c) Cross case syntheses, and (d) Case study evaluations. Case study evaluations can attempt to explain the links between an initiative and its outcomes (Mark, 2008, p. 125; Shavelson & Towne, 2002, pp. 99–110).

The research used narrative, quantitative, and documentary methods.

# APPENDIX F

## *John Kotter's Eight Step Process "Leading Change!"*

**Step 1**: Establishing a Sense of Urgency

> Help others see the need for change and they will be convinced of the importance of acting immediately.

**Step 2**: Creating the Guiding Coalition

> Assemble a group with enough power to lead the change effort and encourage the group to work as a team.

**Step 3:** Developing a Change Vision

> Create a vision to help direct the change effort and develop strategies for achieving that vision.

**Step 4:** Communicating the Vision for Buy-in

> Make sure as many as possible understand and accept the vision and the strategy.

**Step 5**: Empowering Broad-Based Action

> Remove obstacles to change, change systems or structures that seriously undermine the vision, and encourage risk-taking and nontraditional ideas, activities, and actions.

**Step 6:** Generating Short-Term Wins

> Plan for achievements that can easily be made visible, follow-through with those achievements, and recognize and reward employees who were involved.

**Step 7:** Never Letting Up

> Use increased credibility to change systems, structures, and policies that don't fit the vision, also hire, promote, and develop employees who can implement the vision, and finally reinvigorate the process with new projects, themes, and change agents.

**Step 8**: Incorporating Changes Into the Culture

> Articulate the connections between the new behaviors and organizational success and develop the means to ensure leadership development and succession.

# References

Albert, S., & Whetton, D. (1985). Organizational identity. *Research in Organizational Behavior, 7,* 263–295.
All Hallows College (2006). All Hallows College Adult Learning Feasibility Report. Dublin: All Hallows College.
All Hallows College (2006). All Hallows Capital Campaign 2006–2010 Operation Report, Dublin: All Hallows College.
All Hallows College (2008). Ministry with Integrity and Ethical Guidelines for Staff and Students. Dublin: All Hallows College.
All Hallows College (2008). All Hallows College Records Management Policy. Dublin: All Hallows College.
All Hallows College (2008). Linkage Agreement between All Hallows College and Dublin City University. Dublin: All Hallows College and Dublin City University.
All Hallows College (2012). Business and Sustainability Plan 2013-2017. Dublin: All Hallows College.
All Hallows College (2014). Aisling 2017 Strategic Plan. Dublin: All Hallows College.
All Hallows College. (2016). Case study evaluation research project, "Anchoring Cultural Change and Organizational Change." *Case Study Research Evaluation Project, All Hallows College Dublin 1995–2015.* Dublin, Ireland: Author.
American Productivity and Quality Center. (1997). Organizational change, US. *Consortium Benchmarking Study, 21.* Retrieved from www.apqc.org
Bauman, Z. (1990). *Thinking sociologically.* West Sussex, England: Blackwell.

# References

Baumeister, R. (1998). Ego depletion: Is the active self limited resource. *Journal of Personality and Social Psychology, 74*(5), 1252–1265.

Baumeister, R., & Vohs, K. (2003). Does high self-esteem cause better performance, interpersonal success, happiness. *Journal of Psychological Science in the Public Interest, 4*(1), 1–44.

Bolman, L., & Deal, T. (2008). *Reframing organizations* (4th ed.). San Francisco, CA: Jossey-Bass.

Bradshaw, T. (2007). Communities not fazed: Why military base closures may not be catastrophic. *Journal of the American Planning Association, 65*(2), 193–206. http://www.tandfonline.com/loi/ripa20

Bridges, W. (2009). *Managing transitions* (3rd ed.). Cambridge, MA: Da Capo Press.

Bryman, A. (2012). *Social research methods* (4th ed.). Oxford, England: Oxford University Press.

Coleman, J. S. (1974). *Power and the structure of society.* New York, NY: Norton.

Collins, J., & Porras, J. (2005). *Built to last-successful habits of visionary companies.* New York, NY: Random House.

Cummings, T., & Worley, C. (2015). *Organization development and change* (10th ed.). Nashville, TN: Southwestern.

Curran, T. (1983). *A study of the situation in All Hallows in 1983.* Dublin: All Hallows.

Czarniawska, B. (1997). *Narrating the organization.* Thousand Oaks, CA: SAGE.

Dalzell, T. (2014). A brief history of all hallows and some of its more recent presidents. *Colloque, 65,* 15–17.

DiGorgio, R. M., & Associates. (2008). *Discussions among HR staff.* Change Affinity Group. New Jersey Human Resources Planning Society.

Douglass, F. (1886). *Speech.* Retrieved from teachingamericanhistory.org

Dudovskiy, J. (2018, January). *The ultimate guide to writing a dissertation in business studies: A step-by-step assistance* [Ebook]. San Francisco, CA: Goodreads.

Eisenbach, R., Watson, K., & Pillai, R. (1999). Transformational leadership in the context of organizational change. *Journal of Organizational Change Management, 12*(2), 80–89. http://dx.doi.org/10.1108/09534819910263631

Elliott, J. (2007). *Using narrative in social research.* Thousand Oaks, CA: SAGE.

Feldman, M. A. (2002). To manage is to govern. *Public Administration Review, 62*(5), 541–554.

FORFAS (n.d.). National Policy Advisory Board for enterprise, trade, science, technology and innovation. Gov. Publications Dept of Jobs, Enterprise and Innovation, Dublin.

Gibran, K. (1908). *Spirits rebellious.* (W. Jonson, trans.). Indiana Publishing Platform.

Ginsburg, R. (2017). Associate Supreme Court Judge, Speech, United States. Speaking at the "Great Lives in the Law" series. Duke Law School. North Carolina: Duke University.

Hartenbach, W. (1996). Vincentian spirituality. *Vincentian Heritage Journal, 17*(1), Article 4.

Hatch, M. J., & Schultz, M. (2002). The dynamics of organizational identity. *Human Relations, 55*(8), 989–1018.

Hay Leadership Project. (n.d.). Quote from St. Vincent De Paul. Chicago, IL: DePaul University.

Hunt, C. (2010). *National strategy for higher education for 2030.* Dublin, Ireland: Department of Education and Skills.

Ikeda, D. (2009). *Buddhism in action for peace.* Tokyo, Japan: Soka Gakhai International.

Katzenbach, J., Steffen, I., & Kronley, C. (2012, July). Cultural change that sticks: Start with what's already working. *Harvard Business Review.* Retrieved from http://cviewstrategies.com/wp-content/uploads/2014/03/HBR_Cultural-Change-That-Sticks.pdf

King, M. L., Jr. (1957). *Remaining awake through a great revolution.* Speech given at the National Cathedral, Washington, DC.

Kotter, J. (1996). *8 step process in leading change.* Cambridge, MA: Harvard Business School.

Kotter, J. (2012). *Leading change.* Author. (Originally published in 1996)

Kotter, J., & Haskett, J. (1992). *Corporate and performance.* New York, NY: Free Press.

Leary, M. R., & Tangney J. P. (Eds). (2003). *Handbook of self and identity.* New York, NY: The Guildford Press.

Lin, Y. (2004, March). *Organization identity and its implications on organization development.* Research Report Paper presented at the Academy of Human Resource Development International Conference (AHRD), Austin, Texas.

Machiavelli, N. (2012). *The prince* (T. Parks, Trans., & Ed.). London, England: Penguin Books. (Originally published in 1531)

Mandela, N. (2013). *Nelson Mandela quotes.* New Rochelle, NY: African Heritage Press.

Mayo, P. (2008). *Military base closure and community transformation: The case of England Air Force Base in Central Louisiana.* New Orleans, Louisiana: The University of New Orleans.

Mischel, W., & Morf, C. C. (2003). The Self as a psycho-social dynamic processing system: A meta-perspective on a century of the self in psychology in M. R. Leary & J. P. Tangney (Eds). *Handbook of self and identity* (pp. 15–43). New York: The Guildford Press.

Mousin, C. B. (2005). Vincentian leadership—Advocating social justice, De Paul University. *Vincentian Heritage Journal, 26*(1), 254–258.

Nadler, D. (1995). *Disastrous change: Leading organizational transformation.* San Francisco, CA: Jossey-Bass.

Podolny, J., & Phillips, D. (1996). *The dynamics of organizational status.* Oxford: Oxford University Press. https://doi.org/10.1093/icc/ 5.2.453

Pope John Paul II. (1987). *Redemptoris missio* [The mission]. Vatican City: Vatican II Documents.

Pope John Paul II. (1988). *Christifedis laici* [The Lay Faithful]. Vatican City: Vatican II Documents.

Pope John Paul II. (1992). *Pastores dabo vobis* [I will give you shepherds]. Vatican City: Vatican II Documents.

Rafferty, K. (2006). All Hallows 1982–1995: A time of transition. In J. McCormack (Ed.), *All Hallows Studies Summer 2006* (pp. 143–160). Dublin: All Hallows College.

Rao, H., Davis, G., & Ward, A. (2000). Embedness, social identity and mobility: Why firms leave the NASDAQ and join the New York Stock Exchange. *Administrative Science Quarterly, 45*(2), 583–613.

Schein, E. (2010). *Organizational culture and leadership* (4th ed.). San Francisco, CA: Jossey-Bass.

Schön, D. A. (1983). *The reflective practitioner.* New York, NY: Basic Books.

Schramm, W. (1971). Notes on case studies of instructional media projects. In R. Yin (Ed.), *Case study research* (5th ed.; p. 17). Thousand Oaks, CA: SAGE.

Scott, W. R. (2003). *Organizations: Rational, natural and open systems.* Upper Saddle River NJ: Prentice Hall.

Seijts, G. (2013). Good leaders never stop learning. *Ivey Business Journal.* Retrieved from iveybusinessjournal.com/publication/good-leaders-never-stop-learning/

Shavelson, R., & Towne, L. (2002). Features of education and education research. *Scientific Research in Education.* https://doi.org/10.1722/102.36

Sherriton, J., & Stern, J. (1997). *Corporate culture team culture: Recovering hidden barriers to team success.* New York, NY: AMACOM.

St. Augustine of Hippo. (1961). *Confessions.* London, England: Penguin Classics.

Vincentian Family. (2010). Retrieved from https://cmglobal.org/en/vincentian-family/

Whetton, D. (2006). Albert and Whetton revisited: Strengthening the concept of organizational identity. *Journal of Management Inquiry.* https://doi.org/10.1177/1056492606291200

Whetton, D., & Mackey, A. (2000). A social actor conception of organizational identity. *SAGE Journals Business and Society, 41*(4), 393–414.

Yin, R. (2012). *Applications of case study research.* Thousand Oaks, CA: SAGE.

Yin, R. (2014). *Case study research* (5th ed.). Thousand Oaks, CA: SAGE.

Yin, J., & J. Nugent. (1995). Institutions and economic development. In *Handbook of development economics* (Vol. 3, Part 1, pp. 2301–2370). New York, NY: Elsevier Science BV.

Zuckerman, E. W. (1999). The categorical imperative: Securities, analysts and the illegitimacy discount. *American Journal of Sociology, 104*(5), 1398–1438.

Printed in the United States
By Bookmasters